MANIC POP THRILL

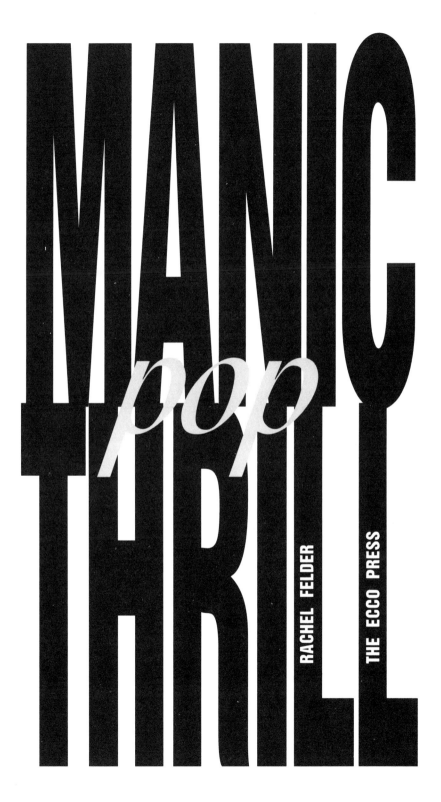

MANIC pop THRILL

RACHEL FELDER

THE ECCO PRESS

Copyright © 1993 by Rachel Felder

The Ecco Press
100 West Broad Street
Hopewell, NJ 08525

Published simultaneously in Canada by
Penguin Books Canada Ltd., Ontario

Printed in the United States of America

Designed by The Typeworks

First Edition

Library of Congress Cataloging-in-Publication Data

Felder, Rachel.
    Manic, pop, thrill / Rachel Felder.
        p.   cm.
    ISBN 0-88001-324-9
    1. Rock groups. 2. Rock music – History and criticism.
3. Popular culture – United States. I. Title.
ML3534.F455   1993
781.66 – dc20   93-36941
                                                       CIP
                                                       MN

The text of this book is set in Cochin

ACKNOWLEDGMENTS

I suppose it's standard to begin your book by thanking your editor. In my case, I should be writing an entire book of thank-yous to my wonder-editor, Jeanne Wilmot Carter. Quite simply, without her support – personal as much as professional – there would be no *Manic Pop Thrill*. To her, Daniel Halpern, and all at Ecco, I'm grateful.

Unlike many music books, my list of acknowledgments doesn't include loads of publicists – or any, for that matter. This is a fan's book, written by one with no outside "write-about-my-band" input. Thanks go, however, for assistance, advice, guidance, and time to: Simon Alexander, Chris Bigg, the Boo Radleys, Lori Carson, Torry Colichio, Brian Cullman, the Dambuilders, dis, Peggy Dold, Peter Crawford, John S. Hall, Matthew Kaplan, Kitchens of Distinction, luna, Joe McEwen, Alan McGee, Vaughan Oliver, Ira Robbins (and his Bible-like *Trouser Press Record Guide*), Paula Rogers, John Silva, Peter Shershin, Joan Snitzer, small factory, David Stamm, Geoff Travis, Robbie Tucker, Unrest, Douglas Wolk, Steve Yegelwel. Special thanks to Richard Grabel, Hal Willner, and my best friend and confidant, RLF.

for my Uncle Doc, who taught me how to care and how to listen

CONTENTS

MANIC POP THRILL

THE ONE ALTERNATIVE MUSIC INDUSTRY

Let's face it: The term "alternative"—which is used more often than not to describe mega-selling bands like R.E.M. and Jesus Jones as well as less than mega-sellers like, say, Tad and Jesus Lizard—is just plain inadequate. I mean, what's called "alternative" is anything but one coherent musical sound; a cross section of alternative bands is as variegated as a UN conference. There is, however, one common denominator which defines this hodgepodge of bands and sounds as alternative, at least for me: a twisting of musical conventions (and so listener expectations) through a variety of musical devices and details. Those devices range from grungy guitars to noise-chamber feedback to top-of-your-lungs anti-vocals; they add interest and originality to what alternative bands do like a new spice in an old-fashioned stew. And because of the unique twists they add to their music, ten alternative bands may not sound anything alike—what

1

lumps them together is simply, in some cases, their rejection and inversion of mainstream musical norms (like, for example, the slick, clean vocals and instruments you'd hear in a typical chart-topping pop record). From the airy delicacy of the Cocteau Twins to the tough bite of Sonic Youth, "alternative" is as polychromatic as the sounds it defines.

And when you think about it, it sure seems weird to deem a band like Nirvana—perhaps the archetypical alternative-band-makes-good—"alternative" after it sold five million copies of its album *Nevermind* in America alone. Relegating the band to some mysterious (ooh! alternative!) rock 'n' roll counterculture seems just plain illogical, as the band has now affected mainstream fashion and culture. And the same could certainly be said of R.E.M, the Cure, Depeche Mode and other bands whose roots are alternative—whatever that means—but sell mass numbers of records, play huge arenas, and attract a broad base of fans.

So the question remains, if Nirvana's realm is alternative, just what is it an alternative to?

Using Nirvana as an example, let's say that question can be answered on a variety of levels. Musically, this band pulls components from everyone from Iggy Pop and his roaring Stooges to the Beatles, synthesizing addictive pop songs through a layer of guitar sludge. There's an almost tangible anger to the sound, as you can hear on the track that broke the band through to a mass audience: "Smells Like Teen Spirit," featuring insistent, snarled guitars and lead singer Kurt Cobain's gruff, smoked-too-many-cigarettes growl. On top-40 radio (or Contemporary Hit Radio—aka CHR—as it's currently called to encompass a typical urban mix of dance music, ballads, and the odd metal-esque big seller), which bases playlists on glossy fare like Mariah Carey and Whitney Houston, the contrasting jolt of Nirvana's sound becomes clear. In the same way that the Sex Pistols' "God Save the Queen" opposed the Abba and Rod Stewart hits it was played between on late-seventies British Radio One, Nirvana clashes from the norm and so offers listeners (aha!) an alternative. On that level, the alternative label works.

That deliberate break from what's become mainstream music establishment brings up the issue of alternative music (the direct descendant of punk) as postmodern entity. In his landmark essay "Postmodernism and Consumer Society," Fredric Jameson says that the two salient, requisite characteristics of postmodernism are that it embodies "specific reactions against the established forms of high modernism" and erodes "the old distinction between high culture and so-called mass or popular culture." According to this definition, Nirvana, along with My Bloody Valentine, the Cocteau Twins, the Jesus and Mary Chain, and virtually every other band discussed in this book are necessarily postmodern. If the nonchallenging sounds of a mainstream artist like, say, George Michael or current-day Eric Clapton or Elton John, are seen as "high modernism" (otherwise known as the once rebellious medium of rock 'n' roll diffused into something easy-to-aurally-digest for the masses), then Nirvana—singing to its peers, growling and roaring and making urgent records with blemishes intact—is a "specific reaction" to it; if rock 'n' roll is assumed to be lightweight disposable music with inaudible, vacuous lyrics (the epitome of popular culture), then alternative bands dealing with serious issues in their music, integrating artwork into their packaging, and often infusing their music with intelligence breaks into the "high culture" realm. In his essay, Jameson lists bands like the Clash and the Gang of Four as embodying the postmodern ethic in their work. Today's alternative bands carry their torch.

To pull Nirvana again as a quick example, the band takes the song structures of pop (they regularly cite the Beatles as an influence in interviews), mixes in the volume and guitar blast of heavy metal, and then twists those elements. By then adding too-intense vocals, too-urgent drums, and lyrics directed at the band's contemporaries, Nirvana processes those conventional components, personalizing them to give them a relevance to its audience. By commenting lyrically on societal problems (everything from senseless murder to teenage peer pressure), the band's lyrics tackle the substantial issues addressed in poetry, fiction, drama, and art—in Jameson's terms, "high culture."

But if we're to really understand alternative music, we can't just pull a current example like Nirvana and start from there; the roots of this music can be found in the punk movement of the late seventies, which shunned the musical conventions of the time. Those conventions can be heard in the slick, overproduced music of seventies records by bands like Genesis, Yes, and Abba, who kept distanced from their fans, released big-budget records, and performed live in huge arenas with light shows and costumes. For those who wanted an alternative to these glitzy bands, nothing could be more different than punk bands like the Sex Pistols and the Clash: working-class guys, garbed in ripped modern-day-urgent clothes, yelling about the political issues that affected them, performing in dank little clubs, making records that captured the frill-free spark of a live bootleg tape. For unemployed, disengaged London kids, punk offered a sound, look, and attitude with which they could empathize.

To concentrate on this dichotomy between punk rock and the top-40 ethic of its day, let's take a band like the Clash. While bands like Genesis featured experienced, rehearsed musicians, the Clash could barely play their instruments; as other groups charmed their audiences with sugar-sweet vocals, singers Joe Strummer and Mick Jones snarled, screamed, and growled nearly atonally. Instead of glitzy stage clothes, the Clash wore ragged, ripped shirts and trousers held together with safety pins, and splattered with multi-colored paint stains à la Jackson Pollock.

Mid-seventies rock was dominated by superstars like Rod Stewart and Elton John, who detached themselves from their audiences, but the Clash presented themselves as average, down-to-earth, "real people," surviving, angry, and struggling just as their fans were. This "Joe Average" stance is crucial; it's the same stance that Nirvana and Dinosaur Jr. and Sonic Youth and so many other alternative bands have taken. In many ways, the top-40 charts circa 1977 are analogous to the top-40 charts circa 1988, 1989, 1990, 1991, 1992; big, manufactured, too-precise music dominates. In the late eighties and early nineties, the top-40 mainstream is still dominated by musicians like Rod Stewart and Elton John (now ten more years older than MTV's teens-through-to-twenties demographic, edging in on the age of those kids' parents) along with the glitz of Paula Abdul and Janet Jackson, the stagey pinup presence of New Kids on the Block, the majored-out traditionalism of a Bryan Adams or John Cougar Mellencamp, and even (as if to drive the point home) remakes galore, from "La Bamba" to Natalie Cole's "Unforgettable" to too many Michael Bolton tracks to mention. And so, Nirvana's growl provides the same jolt as the Sex Pistols' did in 1977: Both offer relief, antithesis, and — here we have it — an alternative to mainstream chart music. The release of albums like *Never Mind the Bollocks: Here's the Sex Pistols* (1977) and *Nevermind* (1991) during economic recession — whether in 1977 England or 1991 America, respectively — is almost painfully appropriate: Their purity and urgency make it seem as if the music is actualizing (if only for your ears) real-life hardships as opposed to affluent glitz.

There are parallels to this pronounced break with the establishment in virtually all the arts: Barbara Kruger and Jeff Koons's artwork, the Starn Twins' photography, Harold Pinter's plays and Joan Didion's novels, the films of everyone from Jean-Luc Godard to Raul Ruiz to Spike Lee. In the late sixties, Liverpool poets Brian Patten, Roger McGeogh, and Adrian Henri wrote in colloquial English and included references to the Beatles and Woolworths to break the notion of poetry as something refined and hard to grasp; contemporary choreographers from Paul Taylor to Twyla Tharp to Mark Morris have rejected the concept of dance as something "tutued balletic" and classical by incorporating popular music and street costumes into their work; Jackson Pollock spizzled paint on his canvas and denied that painting had to be representational or "beautiful." Alternative music makes congruent statements: Pop music doesn't have to be safe and lightweight and disposable—it can roar and seethe with real emotions and problems; it can envelop diverse musical and social influences; it can writhe with addictive fervor. Just as an artist in a nonmusical medium will take a classical base (for Pollock, a standard canvas and oil paints; for Tharp, some ballet movement) and twist it to update and personalize it, so a band like Nirvana uses a Beatlesque device like a catchy, repeated chorus as a base on which to layer its own statements.

And alternative music's expression of a postmodern aesthetic isn't limited to just the sounds alternative bands make: the infiltration of seven-inch vinyl singles on independently owned tiny labels with names like "Slumberland" and "SubPop" is as responsive to the convention of compact discs on multinational conglomerates like Sony and Time Warner as, say, sculptor Haim Steinbach is to more traditional sculptors. In an age of rehearsed and choreographed music videos on MTV, most alternative bands play liver-than-live, lugging guitars and amps to tour a gritty circuit of alternative clubs. And the way fans dress, dance, act—it's all an expression of "fed-upness" with the status quo. What makes alternative music culturally important is about much more than just sound: "Alternative" encompasses a whole ethic. And as bands like Nirvana and Pearl Jam infiltrate the mainstream, the relationship of that ethic to a more mainstream one becomes more complex—and, if you ask me, more interesting.

While the term "postmodernism" has become synonymous with a strict eighties consumerist vibe (it seems like the word conjures up images of overpriced artwork by Julian Schnabel or Jeff Koons sold to a character from the movie *Wall Street*), my use of the word shouldn't: it assumes Jameson's conditions and goes from there. To me, the alternative bands of the eighties and nineties are the aural parallel of Marcel Duchamp's famous toilet seat hung in a museum or Robert Mapplethorpe's mid-seventies photographs of sadomasochistic scenes: brutal, confrontational, controversial, thought provoking. Both contradict past aesthetics without needing to articulate that conflict. If the standard, bland, top-40 pop song is the establishment, then the way that alternative bands twist, warp, and augment the conventions those pop songs use is postmodern; if pop lyrics are supposed to be simple boy-meets-girl stories (in Jameson's terms, popular culture), then the way alternative music deals with everything from social issues to highbrow literature (the territory of high culture) articulates Jameson's postmodern condition of breaking the distinction between high and popular culture.

And if the music business establishment is compact discs slickly produced out of big corporate offices, then vinyl releases on labels like TeenBeat, Slumberland, K, Dark Beloved Cloud, Simple Machines, and Pop Narcotic are the reification of postmodern alternative music. These small labels are run by staffs of one or, at most, a handful; they put out seven-inch vinyl 45-rpm singles, work usually without contracts, and sell to as many specialist shops and fans as possible. As major-labels think in millions and hundreds of thousands, these small self-owned labels usually think in the hundreds. But, because their bottom line is often the simple love of music as opposed to making money, supporting a large staff, fulfilling a long-term contract, and so many other major-label concerns, they can take musical risks most labels simply can't. In other words, these small labels are a breeding ground for music that is alternative.

But let's return to the aural details that make a band alternative. Easy-to-hear examples are the exorcised pound of the Wedding Present's too-fast, too-emphatic non-stop guitars; the drugged-out loop of My Bloody Valentine's miasmic sound; the wispy delicacy of Ride's vocals. All three bands, along with the others discussed in this book, compose traditional, "mainstream" pop songs but warp those songs by superimposing layers and musical details that make them alternative. Bands like the Jesus and Mary Chain and My Bloody Valentine use traditional components like poppy melodies and repeated, hooky choruses as a foundation to their work—but then pervert, pound, personalize those elements to make this music intrinsically postmodern. It's the launch off that base that gives these bands long-term impact on both a musical and a cultural level; it gives their music a substantiality that some alternative bands, working without those referents, seem to lack – and so have not been included in this book. For the most interesting alternative bands (like, say, Sonic Youth), twisting expectations is about more than just music: Just as Sonic Youth's guitars sound less in-tune than you might expect, the dress and attitudes of its members are more aggressive, confrontational, or just plain different than what listeners probably anticipate. The impact of alternative music is not just one of sound and volume; it's as much about who listens and why they listen and what they wear and where they buy it. To really understand alternative music is to understand an entire sociological scene.

The sounds that categorize a record as alternative as opposed to mainstream may, admittedly, vary from band to band, but fans respond almost instinctively to them. They're the sort of qualities that make a fourteen-year-old boy deem a record cool enough to admit to his friends that he listens to it or to advertise his alliance by wearing the band's name on a t-shirt across his chest. With some bands, it's a question of jolting a pop song with layers of rippling guitars; with others, it's washing out the song's edges so it's like a hazy, faded watercolor version of a top-40 hit. And it's the upkeep of those details that has allowed some bands to keep their initial fans while branching out to bigger audiences. In spite of large record and ticket sales, bands like the Cure and Depeche Mode have maintained the weird, left-of-center twists in their work that make them inherently different from a more accessible artist like, say, Bruce Springsteen. Depeche Mode, for example, differs from the average dance band via lead singer Dave Gahan's deadpan voice, the band's arty, leather-clad visuals, which are apparent in their stage presence and videos – it's sort of Robert Mapplethorpe meets Kraftwerk in a spaghetti western – and their somewhat subversive lyrics (as mere titles of songs like "Personal Jesus" and "Master and Servant" suggest).

Certainly, artists like Michael Jackson or Prince also color their work with quirky, trademark gestures, but theirs is a for-the-masses attitude; their music also has a certain almost tangible slickness in production and presentation that alternative performers simply don't have. (Compare, for example, Cure leader Robert Smith's voice with Prince's, and you'll hear what I mean.) Thus, R.E.M. – an alternative entity – on MTV – an un-alternative one – still works apart from the mainstream. The band's continued success on alternative sales and airplay charts (which it shares with the likes of Lou Reed and U2 as well as alternative bands like Kitchens of Distinction and Ned's Atomic Dustbin who have not crossed into mainstream appeal – yet) attests to that.

So, "alternative" can be more about attitude than sales figures; the credibility that a band like Nirvana has maintained with its initial, die-hard fans (what the music industry calls their "fan base") while selling millions of records is the proof. The key to that maintenance is to not alienate those original fans: to still dress like they do, express beliefs they agree with in interviews, play tours alongside other alternative acts. But it's yet more complicated – the alternative scene has its own network of alternative business and media systems: independently owned record labels; independently owned distribution companies to get those records in the shops; independently owned shops (for that matter), which often stock records a big chain like Tower or Musicland might not want to take a chance on; alternatively programmed college radio stations; small magazines called "fanzines"; clubs and small concert halls. Within these systems Nirvana made its first record (*"Bleach"*, on the Seattle-based SubPop label), toured the country, and got some college radio airplay. To get to the next level of sales and popularity, the band had to switch to a major label (DGC, which is part of Geffen, home of huge sellers like Guns 'n' Roses and Aerosmith) distributed by a major distribution company (UNI) so that their records could get into major chains, get promoted to and so played on mainstream radio stations, and get crisp-looking videos made and aired on MTV.

The way Nirvana's fan base exploded with its "Teen Spirit" single through those means questions the validity of the concept of alternative as it specifically codifies music. For Nirvana to really "break big," as music industry lingo would put it, the standard means had to be used: These include everything from media exposure, like being shown on MTV, to promotions, such as in-store appearances in major chains like Tower, to merely being signed to a major label. To sell five million copies, Nirvana had to appeal to record buyers who usually buy heavy metal records, or Whitney Houston records, or whatever mainstream artist they choose. By going outside the "alternative" demographic, Nirvana eased its way into the mainstream. But by sticking to its original alternative guns – by still doing interviews with fanzines, by sustaining its smash-it-up sound, by approaching icons of the rock 'n' roll establishment like (as weird as it may sound to anyone from the sixties) *Rolling Stone* with an adamantly "fuck you" attitude (by wearing a t-shirt reading "CORPORATE MAGAZINES STILL SUCK"), the band affirmed its alternative identity. Which is not to say that other alternative bands haven't done the same; R.E.M. and Jesus Jones, along with bands like Depeche Mode and the Cure, have unquestionably expanded from their initial base through these mainstream media without "selling out" (in other words, without major changes in sound or stance). Nirvana has just done it recently, quickly, and with a lot of chutzpah.

It's important to understand the logistics of alternative systems like college radio and independent labels to get an idea of the alternative scene and how it operates both on its own and in relation to the mainstream media. The music industry has systems through which music is circulated, publicized, played, and sold (in industry terms, "broken"), like radio airplay, press, video markets like MTV, and touring. Over the last fifteen-ish years, the alternative system has evolved—independent labels, college radio, small regional clubs, and a network of small magazines and fanzines (homemade, low-on-production/high-on-fan-driven-content magazines covering a band or group of bands) provide ways for alternative bands to be heard. In the course of that time, this system has become as efficient as, say, the bigger one of DGC and UNI distribution and national chain stores in which Nirvana's *Nevermind* was released. The key to alternative systems—and the true embodiment of the word "alternative"—is that they offer a means of breaking a record outside of mainstream outlets. Each of these systems has a mainstream equivalent: i.e., SubPop or Merge Records versus Warner Brothers or Geffen; *Alternative Press* versus *Rolling Stone*; a local cable show screening videos versus MTV; college radio trade publications such as *CMJ New Music Report* and *Rockpool* versus *Billboard*. To understand the way these systems work is to be able to understand what its bands are in for and up against. And frankly, many people both in and outside of the alternative realm question the relevancy of using the term "alternative" to describe such a broad musical scope. It's the existence of these systems that reinforces the fact that the term "alternative" is about not just sound but an attitude and a lifestyle—that it encompasses where people shop, what they wear when they're shopping, where they hang out, and what they watch on television.

Step one in the recording career of many alternative bands—

excluding the tape or tapes bands make in order to drum up label interest, called a demo tape — is being signed by an independently owned label, referred to by fans and the music industry alike as an "indie." Indies are, in themselves, alternatives; while the bulk of the music business is dominated by labels owned and distributed by America's six major record companies — EMI Record Group North America (which owns SBK, Chrysalis, EMI, Virgin, and others); Warner Brothers (including Sire, Elektra, Atlantic, and others); Sony (encompassing Columbia and Epic Records as well as Sony); MCA (owned by Matshushita and including Geffen and DGC Records); BMG (including RCA and Arista); and PolyGram Label Group (incorporating A&M, Mercury, Island, Polydor, and others) — indies are, as their name implies, owned by an individual or group of individuals instead of a mega-corporation.

In addition, indie rosters are much smaller than major labels do: They have label staffs of, say, ten people instead of five hundred. The acts on their rosters can benefit from the hands-on attention an indie can provide. And as the budgets necessary to make and break an indie record are much smaller than those required for most major-label releases, the indie isn't under the same pressure to sell vast amounts to break even. Thus, indies can be more adventurous than the major companies in their signings.

In addition, indie rosters are much smaller than those of a major label. Many indie labels only release records by a handful of acts; therefore, artists can be prioritized and developed. That care has not gone unnoticed. Major-label a&r people — the staff members who find and sign new artists, whose "a&r" title is an always-used abbreviation for the old term "artists and repertoire" — have tracked and signed bands off indie labels for years. To list a few examples: Nirvana moved from SubPop to DGC, Teenage Fanclub moved to DGC from Matador (which, a couple of years later, signed a deal with major Atlantic), Mazzy Star left Rough Trade for Capitol, the Afghan Whigs went from SubPop to Elektra, Surgery jumped from Amphetamine Reptile to Atlantic, the Poster Children signed to Sire from TwinTone. And the list goes on and on.

Just as independent labels offer bands an alternative to majors, independent distribution companies offer those labels a means to getting their records in the shops without dealing with the majors. (Each major-label group is distributed by its own parent distribution company: CEMA, WEA, Sony, UNI, BMG, and PGD, in respective order from the list of majors above.) These distributors also often own or partially own their own labels, as is the case with Caroline's own imprint label and Dutch East's Rockville and Homestead Records. One of the country's most important indie distributors, Rough Trade America, which also owned an influential label of the same name, folded due to bankruptcy in 1991.

The roots of the cutting-edge indie labels, both in England (from those that started in the early eighties, like 4AD and Mute, to more recent ones like Too Pure and — as its impact really became clear in the early nineties — Creation) and America (SubPop, K, Matador), lie, as do so much of the music they release, in England circa punk's inception and reign: 1976, 1977, 1978. A cluster of independently owned labels, such as Stiff, Rough Trade, and Factory, were launched from humble beginnings: Rough Trade began as an extension of a London record shop; Stiff was started by a concert promoter and a manager, Dave Robinson and Jake Riviera, to release the music they specialized in; the Buzzcocks' seminal *Spiral Scratch* EP was released on the group's own self-financed New Hormones records and became an extraordinarily influential record.

These independent labels paralleled, in a sense, the music they were releasing: just as punk bands were dissatisfied with the mainstream, manufactured fare of the top-40, indie-label owners wanted to offer consumers an option other than glitzy-packaged major-label records. These indies took musical chances a major wouldn't; their humble packaging was totally in sync with the music it contained. The feeling of no-frills immediacy made punk exciting in the way a teenager standing in the front row at a gig idolizing his or her favorite band is excited by the mixture of adrenaline, faith, determination, and sweaty, drunken, no-bullshit passion that is great rock 'n' roll. The same heady formula fuels the archetypical indie label.

It should be noted that England's comparatively small size, its national weekly music press (papers like *NME*, *Melody Maker*, and the now-defunct *Sounds*), and national British Radio One DJ John Peel's support helped these indie labels establish themselves. Today, to have indie records in the British top-20 charts is commonplace, whereas in America, most British indie bands, from Depeche Mode to My Bloody Valentine to the Smiths to the Cocteau Twins, sign to a major label either directly or through a licensing deal between their British label and an American major so that they can tackle the vastness of America with major-label money and muscle.

There are, nonetheless, American indies as well that started in much the same way. Slash grew out of a magazine that covered the bands the label would eventually release. SubPop is an extension of a column on local bands its copresident Bruce Pavitt wrote for a local magazine called *The Rocket*, and Rhino was started by the owner of a record store of the same name. The problem American indies have faced is how to get their records noticed on a national level. Huge chains like Tower and Musicland do not have the same relationship with indie distributors that they do with majors, who can combine several pieces of an alternative record with a big shipment of, say, Bruce Springsteen's latest release. There is no national radio show that all indie music fans listen to. There is no weekly national music paper. Nevertheless, indie labels know how to target their fans: Specific fanzines are appropriate for, say, grunge fans or fans of artier bands like the Cocteau Twins; specific, independently owned record shops cater to techno (sample-heavy dance music), American indie bands like Superchunk and Pavement, cool British imports, or the jangly school of alternative bands from New Zealand. It's the coherence of these fan groups that is one of the main foci of this book.

Alternative records, which, for reasons this book will examine more fully in the chapters that follow, are more subversive or weird or un-immediate or angry or bizarre or theatrical or unpredictable or just plain different from mainstream pop music, have found their audience through their own media. College radio is a prime example of one cog in the alternative system at work: As what's known as alternative music began to flourish in the late seventies and early eighties, the only American radio programmers adventurous enough to play it were at noncommercial college stations. Some college stations service huge urban markets like Boston or Philadelphia and have strong signals; they often are heard by a much broader audience than just university students. As major labels noticed that college stations were appealing to an ever-growing audience, they not only serviced those stations but began to check out their often cutting-edge playlists for bands to potentially sign. Financed by university funding instead of commercials, college radio works outside the commodity system — and so advertiser pressures — of American commercial radio and thus can take those playlist risks.

College radio stations — and their eighteen-to-twenty-two-year-old demographic of alternative record buyers — often have unofficial musical ties to a local alternative music venue and perhaps an alternative record shop. So, for example, many of the bands that are played on WXYC-FM—the University of North Carolina at Chapel Hill's radio station—route their tours to play the Cat's Cradle club there; their records—including vinyl albums and singles—can be found at Schoolkids or Poindexter in nearby Durham. In New Haven, Connecticut, bands play Toad's or the more recently opened Tune-Inn. Kids buy their records at Rhymes and hear them on WYBC-FM, and—I suppose—the lucky ones go to Yale. It's a scenario of interwoven systems that occurs around college centers across the country.

Just as college stations began to offer an alternative to mainstream radio, other ends of the music industry started to develop their own arenas for alternative music. The New Music Seminar was founded in 1980 as an alternative to MIDEM, the mainstream music industry's annual convention in Cannes. South by Southwest and the CMJ Music Marathon, also alternative conventions, were founded soon thereafter. Alternative tip-sheets, such as *Rockpool*, *CMJ*, and *The Gavin Report*, cropped up. These included charts covering the music that *Billboard* didn't. The record industry as a whole has come to acknowledge and respect the impact—and sales potential—of alternative music. For virtually every aspect of the business, there is now an alternative equivalent or specialist, and, in most cases, there are several—all making money. So, there are alternative independent publicists (some with more specific specialties, like industrial or British indie bands), alternative independent radio promoters, and many major labels now have or have had (as is the case with Atlantic) alternative departments.

But there's a key difference between a major label noticing that thousands of people buy alternative records and a guy deciding to create a label to put out his favorite band's first single: While a major corporation is interested primarily in the sales potential of the alternative scene, indie labels are usually fueled by fan-club devotion instead of commerce. Certainly, a tip-sheet or convention devoted to alternative music makes money in the same way, if not on the same scale, in which one dedicated to more mainstream music would. But so many cogs in the alternative machine—college radio DJs, college concert board organizers who book alternative gigs on their campuses, many indie label owners whose financing comes directly out of their own pockets—come from pure love of music.

One of the clearest and keenest examples of a fan-generated

alternative system is the fanzine. Armed with a photocopy machine, an often compulsive knowledge of a band or bands, and a whole lot of enthusiasm, fans put out their own booklets, brochures, or mini-magazines. Sometimes the resulting fanzines are given out free at concerts but, more often than not, they are distributed on a grass-roots level and sold at local record stores and through mail order. Sometimes 'zines have ads, but frequently they don't. And, with titles like *Ablaze*, *Forced Exposure*, *Conflict*, *The Big Takeover*, and *Chick-factor*, they're not quite *Rolling Stone*. But for alternative bands and their potential fans, fanzines are often more relevant and coherent in their coverage than *Rolling Stone* could ever be.

Fanzines are often the first press outlet for alternative bands. They offer artists fervent support publicized to a concentrated, receptive audience with the same focus as a strategically placed ad. Of equal importance is the fact that fanzines write about specific music for specific fans; they offer them a more focused option, an alternative, if you will, to *Rolling Stone*, which covers a broader musical spectrum to reach more readers. But just because fanzines cover a specific type of music doesn't necessarily mean their readership is forever limited. In the same way that a band like Nirvana grew through their alternative base to a wider one, some fanzines, like *Alternative Press* and *B-Side*, have grown to have glossy covers, a full staff of writers, and national and international distribution.

Regionally, fanzines work as part of the local alternative network: the cool college station, the one local club booking alternative bands, the record shop that stocks indies. The entire network caters to alternative fans. That network often services more than just musical tastes: There is usually a hip clothing shop, an alternative bookstore, a cafe. There are also, almost necessarily, local bands both influenced by their surroundings and playing within them; such is the case in Seattle (with bands like Nirvana, Pearl Jam, Mother Love Bone), Providence (home of Velvet Crush and small factory), Washington D.C. (the base for Unrest, Tsunami, and Velocity Girl), and Portland, Oregon (where Pond is from). A new crop of independent labels—like Moist, K, Dischord, TeenBeat, and Slumberland—have cropped up to service local bands. Often, these labels are run by band members; just as often, they release seven-inch vinyl singles. One label, D.C.-based Simple Machines, publishes a pamphlet guide on how to start your own label and even provides a phone number for advice. Some independently-released bands, like Providence's small factory and Chapel Hill's Superchunk, have put together their own festivals of bands—basically a weekend of back-to-back, noon to middle-of-the night gigs—to spotlight their regional scenes. To return to the notion of alternative music as a postmodern, punky reaction to the mainstream music sound and attitude, self-released vinyl in the age of the compact disc is the difference, when you come down to it, between Nirvana and Madonna.

That dichotomy between alternative and mainstream—which, actualized by either a vinyl single bought in a small record shop or a CD bought at a big national chain, you can hold in your hands—is crystal clear to the audiences of both: Maybe most fans can't articulate the difference between the two, but Nirvana makes the listeners' ears and stomach and legs do something different than Madonna does; it makes you put on a different t-shirt and slam dance at a gig instead of voguing or sitting or whatever people do at a Madonna concert. Madonna's just an easy, immediate example (as, I suppose, is Nirvana). The guts of the matter is that "alternative" music—for lack of a better word—gives people a choice, and as more and more people lose patience with the manufactured world of music videos and mega-hype and slickly produced top-40 music, an alternative is exactly what they want. And the alternative choice stretches further than just music: It opts for big, sturdy, unisex Doctor Marten boots over less utilitarian footwear; it says men can wear earrings and noses can be pierced without sending a message other than "I'm cool"; it throws together a variety of seemingly disparate clothing elements depending on fans' and bands' musical tastes. By rejecting and questioning accepted musical norms, alternative bands speak to listeners who feel equally unfulfilled by those norms. By rejecting fashion and behavioral norms, kids use "alternative" to represent a lifestyle as much as a sound.

As music videos have become such an important aspect in bands' presentation of themselves to the public and live shows have become sweetened (or tainted, if that's the way you look at it) by lipsyncing and splashy dance numbers, alternative bands have continued to play live, spreading the word through regular, unadulterated touring. And so, while those other bands (like, say, New Kids on the Block or M. C. Hammer) are about show biz, alternative bands are about reality: schlepping around in a tour van, meeting fans, playing their music—warts and all—regularly. One reason I've left out any examination of music videos in this book is that virtually every alternative band I discuss has toured extensively. That touring has been focused around the frill-free integrity of honest, live musicianship (as opposed to the show biz theatricality of a live show by a performer like Madonna or Michael Jackson). To include an in-depth examination of music videos—usually put together by a video director and a record label's marketing department, often with little band input— would miss the mark with alternative music. Alternative music is about connecting with fans and being close to them, not about the superficiality of staged videos.

Mainstream performers like George Michael distance themselves from their fans: They present themselves from a stadium stage or in a video, where their fans cannot come too close. They wear glitzy costumes (for George Michael, it's Gianni Versace couture) and are seen at fancy restaurants. It's as if modern pop stars are vintage Hollywood glamour queens. In sharp contrast, alternative bands hang out with their fans before and after shows and perform at small clubs where fans can jump on stage and jump back into the audience (otherwise known as stage-diving); they wear the humble clothes their fans do even after they've made it big. That anti–distanced-star ethic is rooted in 1970s punk. But unlike the somewhat limited commercial appeal of punk in the United States, huge numbers of people buy alternative records. And these people (who propelled bands like the Cure and Depeche Mode and created the foundation of support that enabled R.E.M. and Jesus Jones to eventually have a place on charts next to more mainstream artists) not only buy records, they buy t-shirts, they go to clubs to see bands, they buy certain newspapers (like New York's *Village Voice*, Seattle's *Rocket*, and *Boston Rock*) to find out which bands are playing and where. Although alternative fans can be subdivided, they are a thriving, money-spending demographic.

More important, they're people who simply, almost necessarily embrace the bite and passion and integrity of the alternative realm. They're kids—who, in my view, are not determined by age but by ethic—who aren't being addressed by more mainstream music and the fashion/ethic/ideology it represents. They're kids who need a release and are finding it only in alternative music and its larger implications.

MIASMA TWO BANDS

Miasma. The word itself brings up images of an amorphic, blurry, no-distinct-edges glob of stuff. What I call miasma bands—and what other people have called everything from shoegazers to the scene with no name—superimpose the same hazed-out lack of concrete, sharp edges on top of their songs. Sort of the aural equivalent of a soft-focus lens on a camera, miasma music starts with a plain old pop song but layers it underneath whooshy, valiumed guitars, feedback, and impossible-to-pin-down vocals that are often buried beneath enough guitar noise to change their value in the mix from the focal point (as on a Whitney Houston record) to a mere equal-valued component (as if what would be a "lead" vocal is an extra guitar or another set of drums). It's no coincidence that on a recent tour of America by My Bloody Valentine—a pivotal band because they so strongly influenced the whole pied-piper "shoegazing" movement that hit England in 1990 and 1991 – the band performed much of the set in front of an out-of-focus, pinkeye-pink slide of a tunnel, fuzzy to the point of confusion.

Miasma bands clearly illustrate the way alternative groups take existing musical norms (like verse/verse/chorus/verse song structures and hook-based tunes) and twist them. The music of these bands is not necessarily more important than that of, say, American guitar bands, but I discuss it first because it demonstrates "alternative-ness" so well.

Miasma bands sonically actualize the sort of confusion and lack of controlled boundaries that is modern life. I'd better explain: Life circa 1989, 1990, 1991 for miasma fans – really, for just about everybody – was about the buildup to a recession, growing concerns about the planet and the need to recycle, the Gulf War, the threat of AIDS. In other words, feelings of fear, loss, insecurity were all around. It makes sense that so many music journalists dubbed miasma bands "shoegazers": Many of these musicians stare at the ground while they play and, hey, if you had to face those heavy problems, you'd probably hang your head down as well. It's not that miasma bands express all these negative emotions, but that the (pleasing) lack of hard edges in the music, its spaced-out quality, parallels the sort of, well, miasma we all go through to make decisions and even just to survive.

The miasmics deal with world issues not lyrically but sonically – they subvert the directness of a song by raising guitar volume hyperbolically, adding feedback so those guitars are never clear or unfuzzed, squashing vocals deep down in the mix, extending instrumental bridges in songs ad infinitum. It's as if every rule in the "how to perform and produce a song" book is reversed and rewritten. It's as if you're listening to a more traditional pop record on drugs.

And that issue of drug use is no small point. Some of the musicians in miasma bands, like some percentage of what seems like every social group in the world today, do drugs to deal with and so escape life's pressures. But whether you're stoned or not, miasma music is like drugs: It actualizes the blur of drugs, the hazy boundaries between chorus and verse, the almost trapped feeling of layers and layers of insistent, won't-let-up guitars. If punk, ever-pounding and direct, is speed, then the miasmics are hallucinogens – making listeners mellow, trippy, sometimes confused, often nonactive.

It's also important to note that the main influence behind the miasma bands—the Velvet Underground—was equally inspired by drug use. Just as the whirry fog of My Bloody Valentine albums like *Isn't Anything* and *Loveless* seem to aurally actualize a drugged-out listener's loss of focus, so vintage Velvet tracks—hazy Nico-sung languors like "Femme Fatale" and "I'll Be Your Mirror" or spastic blasts of guitar like "Heroin"—equally embody a drugged-out state. For both the Velvets and the miasmics, drugs are not about a peace-and-love hippie vibe or a washed-out passivity. Drugs—or the musical replication of them—are the only way they see to deal with the overload impeti of modern life, be it circa 1967 or circa 1991.

There are, of course, other antecedents, from the psychedelic scrawl of early Pink Floyd to, even more distantly, the echo chamber hugeness of Phil Spector's trademark wall of sound. But both Pink Floyd and Phil Spector work more conventionally than the Velvets do; neither bites like the Underground. When it comes down to it, the Velvets' mix of drugged-out aura, black-leather coolness, guitar noise, and low-fi feedback is the key to Miasma 101.

The gnarled squelch of feedback in songs like the Velvets' "Heroin" is melodramatic, in-your-face, and best heard numbingly loudly. Oddly, however, there's also an almost arty, cool elegance about it. The Velvets' ties to the art world are clear. Pop artist Andy Warhol produced their debut album and also painted its banana-faced cover. The miasma bands, for the most part, don't have such heavy art school ties. But the grandness, the sonic majesty of the haze, is as uplifting—if you're into it—as a commanding, elegant baroque painting or an ornate cathedral.

It's also as imposingly mood-altering as dropping acid, and that's really the point: The music of the Velvets, the Valentines, and the bands that have followed in their wake scrambles and confuses conventional musical borders (like structured guitar lines and bridge lengths). It's as if you're listening to a "normal" rock song while you're strung out on LSD. Just as a drug like acid intensifies and muddles reality, miasma music (from an antecedent like the Velvet Underground's self-titled third album to My Bloody Valentine's *Isn't Anything* to the Boo Radleys' *Everything's Alright Forever*) takes rock 'n' roll conventions and fuzzes them, exaggerates them, bends them out of shape like a stretchy rubber doll. And, let's be honest: Witnessing and experiencing the modern world often feels like you're watching the TV news on drugs. The cacophony of the world's problems in a high-tech age seems like a hyperbolic mirage—or, maybe more accurately, a hyperbolic nightmare. The miasmics' technique of twisting conventions musically articulates (not lyrically, mind you, but *musically*) the frustrations and confusions of modern life.

But there's a paradox at work here: If we accept that life is as confusing as a drug trip, then it's ironic that miasmic music offers simultaneous escape and articulation of that confusion. Somehow, these bands offer a refuge from the world's problems but always point toward them. It's as if the underlying message at a My Bloody Valentine concert is, "Yeah, we know it's tough out there, let's shake it out of ourselves with volume and feedback and anti-harmonies." It's easy to claim that the attitude of togetherness is something fans at any rock show share; but unlike, say, Bruce Springsteen fans, alternative fans usually look different or have different ideological views than mainstream America and so cling to their fellow alternative fans and bands even more.

Other artists in different media also use their work to represent both a refuge and reflection of the bewildering modern world. In Michelangelo Antonioni's mid-sixties film *Red Desert,* a similarly apocalyptic view of the world is portrayed. In this film, the modern world is cold, harsh, and filled with dark machines; simultaneously, the main characters' home — a seeming oasis — is equally bewildering, gloomy, and apocalyptic. Wherever they are, the characters are always off-kilter and slightly lost. Hanif Kureishi's film *London Kills Me* shows the effect of drugs on disinterested, fucked-up kids and the "family" those kids create of and for themselves that is similarly fucked up. Artist/photographer Sandy Skoglund literally constructs an askew oasis of radioactive-green fish and cats, places them in an average-looking home setting, and then photographs them to express the way the world's problems have seeped into the refuge of our homes. As reflected in the sound of the Valentines' splattery guitars, there is not even escape in escape.

And so, while some critics, particularly in America, have dubbed the miasmics' sound "dream-pop," "nightmare-pop" might be more like it. Certainly, the fog of a dream is one element in the music, but fueled by feedbacky, off-kilter guitars, that fog is one of a bleak, confusing, bottomless pit. As dark as the music can sometimes feel, the point of what miasma bands do is to superimpose fuzzed-out details over pop songs, to twist expected "norms," to take what's accepted, mutating it into something personal. In other words, they take what could be mainstream and, through the way they present it, make it alternative.

As so much of the miasma movement is based in England, it's worth pointing out that the school of bands that preceded the miasmics were bands like the Happy Mondays and the Stone Roses. These bands mixed pop tunes beneath dance beats; their fans attended raves: big, anonymous dance parties where drugs and disorientingly loud music went hand in hand. Many of these premiasmic bands came from Manchester, situated in heavily unemployed northern England. The point of enjoying bands like the Mondays was to get, as the British put it, out of your head—to take so many drugs you escape your reality. The miasmics aren't so much concerned with getting away from their problems as with somehow articulating them: actualizing angst and bewilderment with grizzled guitars instead of heavy lyrics. While the Mondays' music is about dancing, the Valentines' is concerned with volume and guitar distortion. Strictly speaking, the latter is more firmly based in the rock tradition, but because it takes rock conventions and turns them on their sides. For many fans, the Valentines and the slew of bands they influenced were a reaction to bands like the Roses and the Mondays, who were very visual and dance-oriented and as accessible, in their own way, as, say, a Debbie Gibson or a Paula Abdul.

My Bloody Valentine and the jumble of bands it has inspired are predominantly British, but there are American bands that have also combined guitar slur with poppy songs and sometimes murky or wispy vocals. The prime example is Galaxie 500, a band composed of three Harvard grads with two Rough Trade albums—*Today* (released in 1988) and *This Is Our Music* (released in 1990)—along with an earlier album, *On Fire*, which was released by Aurora Records. Their music veers closer to a Velvet track like "Sunday Morning" than "I'm Waiting for the Man" (translation: It saunters instead of growls) but still soars with the musical components—a disconcerting, Les Pauled, imposing grind, a no-frills, imperfect-but-not-bothered-by-its-imperfections vocals, and a nonstop rhythmic drawl—of the vintage Underground.

But while Galaxie 500's records are sonically clean productions of Velvet-influenced music, the body of My Bloody Valentine's work which set off the miasma bands, beginning with their 1988 release *Isn't Anything* (along with, it must be said, its preceding British-only EP,° *You Made Me Realise*) is a transliteration of the Velvets' cloudy

°An EP is a record format that is longer than a single and shorter than an album. Generally, EPs run four to six songs. (The letters, incidentally, stand for "extended play.") Although the format was used by bands like the Beatles in the sixties, the EP

aural fuzz. Again, there are songs underneath it all, but "all" is feedback, backward-looped tapes, distortion, endless guitars, and a furtive, near-buried vocal that distorts those songs in the same way, to pick up the visual metaphor again, a wide-angle or soft-focus lens on a camera would distort images.

Another key influence on the Valentines was A. R. Kane, whose two albums, *69* and *i* (both released in England on Rough Trade; chunks of both were compiled on Luaka Bop's *Americana* compilation), combine a pop sensibility (on tracks like "A Love from Outer Space" and "Miles Apart") with the meandering, it-doesn't-have-to-be-three-minutes-or-even-have-lyrics structure of jazz. Juxtaposing those more structured tracks with more ethereal, lingering ones (like "Baby Milk Snatcher" and "Up"), the band's albums stride between different moods and musical genres: Just when you think you've pegged the sound, it bounds into another musical realm. Many of A. R. Kane's songs—like the tracks off the import *Lollita* [*sic*] EP—fuzz into a kind of foggy guitar wash. Almost like a whitewashed take on a conventional instrumental bridge, that layer of haze is also part of the Valentines' sound; and although the Valentines' overall sound is spikier and more frenzied than A. R. Kane's, the music is basically analogous.

Although My Bloody Valentine—or the Valentines or MBV, as the band is often called in the powerful British music press—has made foggy delirium a key component of its music, it wasn't always that way. The band was formed in 1983 by Kevin Shields (who produces the band's records, plays lead guitar, and is the mastermind behind the sound) and Colm O'Ciosoig, the drummer. The band bounced through a variety of band members before settling on the haunting-voiced Bilinda Butcher (who also plays guitars) and bassist Deb Googe in 1987. At the start, they had a fast-paced snarl like that of an Australian band of the early eighties, the Birthday Party (Shields himself has compared his band's first incarnation to this group). As the band began to evolve, Butcher's airy vocals added a new twist. Now, the band could combine gruff guitars with more delicate singing in the same way the Velvets did with Nico tracks like "Femme Fatale." This period of its work is captured on singles like "Sunny Sundae Smile" and "Strawberry Wine." Both cuts combine jangly guitars and those girly vocals with the buoyance of a vintage

play.") Although the format was used by bands like the Beatles in the sixties, the EP format, which can be used on vinyl, cassette, or CD, is a frequent one in the alternative world.

Miasma in action: My Bloody Valentine's Kevin Shields

Shirelles track. (These singles were released by Lazy Records in England. Lazy reissued their tracks from that period as a mini-album called *Ecstasy and Wine*, which came after the 1988 release of *Isn't Anything*.)

My Bloody Valentine jumped to a bigger indie, Creation Records, headed by Alan McGee, to produce its meatiest work. McGee was the first manager of the Jesus and Mary Chain, another key band of the period that both influenced and reflected what the Valentines and the miasma bands were doing (and are the pivotal "feedback" band, addressed in Chapter 7). He is also a visionary who later released many of the miasma bands the Valentines influenced, like Swervedriver, Slowdive, and the Boo Radleys.

On Creation, the band came into its own. Its members smudged the girl group vocals from joyous to haunting and added onion-layers of feedback. The first Creation LP, *Isn't Anything* (which was licensed, for the standard reasons of improved distribution, press, and promotion, to Relativity Records), showcased that new style. It's unfair to generalize an across-the-board formula of femininity mixed with grit on that album; first of all, Kevin still sings lead on tracks like "Cupid Come." But the key to the album is its courageous blend of pop song structures (as on "Feed Me with Your Kiss"), revved-up guitars, and transient, often disconcerting, spacey details. Sometimes it's the mix of Kevin's and Bilinda's voice that accomplishes that device, sometimes it's the fuzzy guitars at the end of a song; sometimes it's an almost out-of-tune tune. This combination is probably best exemplified by the album's "Nothing Much to Lose."

Often the album sounds like a cloudy dream, as on "All I Need"'s pumping heartbeat and amorphic loops; often it sounds somber, almost apocalyptic, as on the grim "No More Sorry." That's what the miasma's about: a cloud that you can't exactly pinpoint but that throws you for a loop. Again, the relevance of that miasma is that its blur is as jolting, disturbing, and shake-you-up confusing as modern life. Miasma's perversion of traditional pop elements—girly harmonies, sweet guitars—actualizes the sometimes perverse standards of the world at the end of the twentieth century—the decaying ozone layer, politicians in sex scandals, AIDS—without ever needing to spell it out. While the miasmics have a specific sound, the reality of the twist is the common denominator of alternative music—even though each subgenre uses a different twist.

It's important to address the issue of the women in the band and what they represent – or, perhaps more correctly, what they don't represent. On the tour that accompanied the release of *Isn't Anything*, the band's female members zealously, with true strength, ripped through their guitar parts without ever breaking into the more usual female stage clichés (coy, flirty, delicate, or even, antithetically, the macho stance of a Joan Jett or Suzi Quatro). On stage as on record, guitars are never delicate or "girly"; and while Bilinda Butcher's vocals do have a haze, they are never vulnerable or fluffy. And it's not that the Valentines' female presence is unsexy or unfeminine – it's that it is anti-sexy, a-feminine. In other words, the attitude is one of thorough equality.

The roots of that attitude can be seen in punk and punk-influenced bands like the Slits and the Au Pairs, who focused on sound rather than a preconception that female bands had to be sweet and lovely and lyrically helpless like, say, the Ronettes or the Supremes. For both of the former bands, and so the Valentines ten years later, feminism isn't about attending rallies and burning bras – it's about obvious equality and an "it goes without saying" sense of power. The Slits posed topless smeared with mud on the cover of their *Cut* LP. The image is not one of sex but rather of an I-dare-you-to-comment defiance, a defiance that is found in their criticism of standard female roles in songs like "Typical Girls." The Au Pairs' female lead, Lesley Woods, taunts men to live up to their clichéd societal roles of sexual aggressor and satisfier in songs like "Repetition" and "Come Again" on their deliberately titled *Playing with a Different Sex* LP. Both bands imply that women can be as musically powerful as men and that being in a girl group (Au Pairs was, and the Valentines are, half male, half female) doesn't mean that bubble gum has to be the end product.

But the Valentines' deliberate neglect of exploiting the femininity of its members goes one step further than the defiant attitudes of those earlier groups. By ignoring the issue, they make it seem irrelevant, and that's the point: If the women in a band are effective players, what does their sex matter, anyway? This stance contrasts with that of performers like Kim Gordon from Sonic Youth and Babes in Toyland's Kat Bjelland, who take female stereotypes and deliberately twist and negate them. My Bloody Valentine's women turn a blind eye to those stereotypes from the start. For the Valentines, who are part of a generation (as, notably, are their fans) who grew up not having to worry about abortion rights and a stigma attached to women working, fighting for women's rights was their parents' problem. So bands like My Bloody Valentine – along with a slew of bands with female members such as Smashing Pumpkins, the Poster Children, the Pale Saints, and many others – can effortlessly have strong female guitarists who are not buying into the frothy, new wave girl-group lightness of bands like the Bangles and the Go-Go's. The female half of the Valentines shouldn't really be labeled as such – they're members, plain and equal.

That said, the visual force of the Valentines' female members still makes an impact. The band makes no concessions to rock-chick clichés; both Butcher and Googe chug at their guitars with a ferocity and physical strength many male players don't have. The result on stage – as was seen on the U.S. tour to support *Isn't Anything* – is admirable and a touch offputting; the message is, "we're female, so what? the bottom line is the music." While other bands of the period – like, say, the Darling Buds or the Primitives – featured a softer, sweeter female presence and voice, the Valentines paired that sweetness with the no-bullshit oomph of its players, regardless of their sex. Attention is never paid to whether or not either woman is attractive or sexy, and, for this generation, rightly so – it's a band of musicians creating music and the sex appeal of its members, male or female, is, in this case, irrelevant.

This gender-oblivious attitude affected the band's fans and, in the long run, the slew of bands they influenced. A couple years after the release of *Isn't Anything*, when the Valentines' influence was being felt via bands like Slowdive and Ride, British fans – female and male alike – wore the same uniform: extra-large t-shirt, preferably long-sleeved, jeans and fringy, mid-lengthed hair. Makeup, skirts, and high heels were not part of the female uniform (compare this fashion statement to, say, the hyper-teased hair and skintight miniskirts in a heavy metal show's ladies' room mirror). As with the white lips and short cropped hair of the sixties original Mods, there is an element of anti-femininity in the look; but what it represents, like the Valentines' female guitarists, is a focus on unity and musicality rather than sexuality.

There is also something metaphorically parallel about the way the music clouds the lines between distinct guitars and feedback, each layer of vocals, choruses, and verses, and the lack of distinction between male and female fashion. Both music and image have the feeling of a cacophonous jumble, and both have a utilitarian toughness. Like grunge fans, miasma fans' long-sleeved t-shirts, dirty hair, and jeans are sturdy and cheap—survivalist wear for a survivalist era. And if spacing out, actualizing confusion with entwined guitars, revving them up to hyperbolic volumes, and goring them with feedback is the way to auralize survival tactics, then de-sexing clothing, turning it into an easy, interchangeable uniform, is the way to wear them.

The way miasma fans dance—almost nondancing, nodding their heads, seemingly transported, druggily nodding-off—is an autonomic reaction. If alternative music fashion is asexual, unfashion, then that minimal-movement dancing is nondancing. But, of course, it's nondancing just as Marcel Duchamp's urinal in a museum is non-art.

The complex, sophisticated blends of *Isn't Anything* left the ever-fickle British rock press fawning. After all, here was an amalgamation of many catalystic sounds that had them raving in the past: the electrified strum of a classic guitar band, the seductive vocals of someone like Debbie Harry from Blondie, the feedback of the Jesus and Mary Chain (more on that later), and the druggy stupor of vintage Pink Floyd. The Valentines' hybrid might sound bizarre on paper, but it is unavoidable—even if you don't like it—on record.

As the Valentines continued to evolve, the band needed more time in the studio—by all accounts, more time for Kevin Shields to experiment with and perfect his style. Creation signed a deal with Sire Records licensing the Valentines, along with two other Creation bands, Primal Scream and Ride, for North American releases so those bands could reach bigger American audiences than Creation could reach on its own on an import basis. The money from that deal helped finance that time and, happily, didn't influence the sound of the bands; it just enabled their records to have adequate budgets, promotion, and distribution. The first results were EPs: *Glider* and *Tremolo*. Like a girl group on hallucinogens, the Valentines now slurred sweet, feminine vocals into an amorphic sludge. As an example, take *Tremolo*'s "Honey Power": Surging guitars rip open the track but are combined with weird, Sergeant Pepper-ed tape loops; verses are wispily sung by Butcher (part Marvellettes, part Nico), but they are always intercut—like a 16mm avant-garde film by someone like Jonas Mekas or even circa–late sixties Jean-Luc Godard—with that emphatic, raging guitar. Splices of sentences are almost intelligible, but not quite. The song has as many elusive elements as pinpointable ones.

Tremolo's next track, just to allude to the way the Valentines' music bops from one mood to the next, is "Moon Song," sung just as wispily by Shields. The drug analogy for this track is Valium: It's as lazed-out and hazy as the soft-focused pink cover of the EP. Still, standard song structures are used; it's just that the band's approach is anti-standard. It's as if your ears are listening to a conventional pop song but are too drugged out to make out distinct harmonies or musical borders. Whether or not the band is on those drugs is irrelevant; the music suggests them and implies that, even if you're not on drugs, life is as bewildering and out-of-control as it would be if you were.

That twisting of accepted boundaries, whether they be proportions of vocals to guitars or feedback added to fuzz those guitars, is, of course, the key to postmodern art. The twist parallels the work of an archetypical postmodern artist like Cindy Sherman, who comments on artifice and superficiality by constantly mutating herself in front of her own camera. By warping everything from B-movie stills to Renaissance paintings, shooting ever-new images of herself through the very modern medium of a high-tech camera, Sherman puts a spanner in what the viewer expects to see in those images in much the way that the miasma bands blur the edges of traditional pop structures. A similar parallel can be seen in Jeff Koons's deliberately tacky, controversial, but also impeccably crafted sculptures of giant Hummel figures and a white Michael Jackson. These works fulfill the requirements Fredric Jameson outlines in his definition of postmodernism, where the breakdown of the distinction between high art versus low art is a rejection of the accepted forms of "high modernism" itself.

It's not that the Valentines' music should turn into a springboard for an intense "postmodernism in alternative music" rant; to get at what the music represents beyond just the way it makes your ears and stomach feel, it's important to recognize what it accomplishes beyond beauty and noise.

Nineteen ninety-one saw the release of the Valentines' most sophisticated work to date, its most effective (and affecting) combination of blissful beauty and miasmic blur: *Loveless*. While some tracks, like the album's opener, "Only Shallow," and "To Here Knows When" have an immediate accessibility, the bulk of the album rejects standards like distinct song endings and beginnings or brief song lengths. Another distinctive mutation from the norm is the way the vocals are mixed into each track — deep, deep under layer after layer of guitars, loops, feedback, and drums. Whereas on a normal pop record, vocals are the easy-to-latch-on-to highlight, on *Loveless* they become merely one equal component of an overall sound. If alternative music is the alternation of accepted musical elements to provide listeners and musicians a choice beyond the norm, then this is it.

Listening to the Valentines' work from *Isn't Anything* onward, you might decipher snippets of songs, lyrics, and harmonies, but just when you've caught it, like a bar of soap in a bathtub, it slips straight out of your grasp. And so the band forces its audience to alter its expectations. Just as viewers of avant-garde films by the likes of Stan Brakhage or Jon Jost are pushed to throw out their anticipation of a neat, narrative beginning, middle, and end, so My Bloody Valentine fans are forced to discard accepted notions of songs' having distinct borders of chorus-verse-chorus structure, intelligible, upfront vocals, clear endings, etc. It's as if they're telling fans to tune in, turn off, space out.

Ever since its *Isn't Anything* LP was released, the band's live shows have been as much about hyperbolically loud volume as about the music itself. That volume heightens their music's intensity as well as adding to the painful disorientation of it—it's so loud, you feel completely dazed. The audience's experience at a Valentines show recalls what Roland Barthes wrote in his essay "Musica Practica," where he discusses the intensity of musical connection you get from playing an instrument yourself and defines it as something intrinsically different from the experience of passively listening to music. The Valentines—along with many of their contemporaries, not just miasmics but volume-heavy guitar bands like Dinosaur Jr. and Sonic Youth—bridge that gap between musician and listener. The volumes at which they play live allow the music to affect the listener corporeally—it's as if, involuntarily, you're literally, physically part of the performance of the music. On stage, the band provides every audience member with that intensity; the volume has an invasive quality—it pulls you in whether you like it or not; you feel your heart beating and your ears ache. You're not merely watching—you're immediately part of the music. The music involves the listener in the same way, by different means, that a point-of-view shot pulls the viewer into a scene in a movie.

And it could certainly be argued that, at least today, the best music, the most moving music, removes that distinction between performer and audience. It seems to me that the accessibility of Bruce

Springsteen or Nirvana or Wedding Present or My Bloody Valentine is enhanced by their everyman-ness. The removal—à la 1977 punk rock—of the distinction between lofty star performer and average guy affords listeners a strong connection to these bands. In the world of virtually every band in this book, fans and musicians look the same, act the same, and have the same kind of experience. This, in my mind, is an absolute expression of postmodernism. Postmodernism is about unanimity between artist and audience, and the visceral quality that the extra-loud volume provides merely intensifies that unanimity.

By the time *Loveless* came out near the end of 1991, England had been bombarded with Valentine-derivative bands for over a year. Its two powerful weekly music papers, *New Musical Express* and *Melody Maker*, were filled with their praises. These bands often go by single-word, obtuse names like Slowdive, Swervedriver, Curve, Lush, and Ride; they have each built from the Valentines' formula of fuzz, volume, and underlying pop song to different degrees of success. To be more specific, both Ride albums are, to me, reasonably classic pop records. The Slowdive album, *Just for a Day*, is interesting for about that long. The British press, while picking up on all these bands' most direct influence, was also eager to give them—and their "scene," which was, to a great extent, also created by that press—a name: "shoegazers." It's a logical name if you've seen any of these bands live: Like MBV, their concentration on stage is on music rather than glamour, so instead of looking ahead at the audience, band members look down at their guitars and, ostensibly, their feet. Another moniker was "the scene with no name," the potency of which was, I think, best summed up by Kitchens of Distinction drummer Dan Goodwin on stage at London ULU in October 1991 when he redubbed it "the scene which gives itself head." In other words, call it what you will, we're basically talking about a group of bands who share influences, an overall sound, and a populist attitude.

The specific details of each band's sound are notably different. Swervedriver, on the one hand, adds a churning Dinosaur Jr./Sonic Youthed—and so American influenced—bite to the mix. On its own debut album, *Raise,* and the British EPs that preceded it, Swervedriver blends the Valentines' fuzz with the revved-up buzz of bands like the Stooges (not to mention more recent bands which tip their musical hats at the Stooges, like Soundgarden). The result is more straight-ahead rock than MBV. On the other hand, Chapterhouse adds a heavy dose of Cocteau Twins influence to loopy guitars and samples and puts it over fogged-out pop songs on their album *Whirlpool*; when it works (on tracks like "Pearl"), it's trippy, bubbly, and sticks almost irrationally in your head.

Slowdive has a different take on the sound, bringing it back to its initial grounding in the Velvet Underground's guitar-wash-frazzle, building the sound around a pale-voiced female vocalist, Rachel Goswell, and washing it out to a lethargic pulse. Ride, on the other hand, adds a focused, spot-on guitar sensibility to the Valentines' haze on its debut album, *Nowhere*. By the time its follow-up, *Going Blank Again*, was released in 1992, the band had refocused its songwriting from somber to almost-buoyant, and so their records got the added spin of being pop-accessible as well.

Swervedriver, Slowdive, and Ride all share the same indie record label, Creation (their records are licensed in America to A&M, SBK, and Sire, respectively). They also share an attitude about songwriting that explores another aspect of what is alternative. While classic pop songs feature lyrics—albeit sometimes singsong lyrics—the miasmics' lyrics are obscured by a slur of production and performance that renders them almost unrecognizable. They are often mixed deep in a wash of guitars so that, admittedly, they are on the nondescript side. And even if you can understand the words, it's not only the sound of these bands' songs that are miasmic; the lyrics themselves are obtuse. The songs have titles like "Vapour Trail," "Seagull," "Sunset," "Waves," and "Primal." It's as if the lyrics are more suggestions of ideas than full-fledged stories or concepts. In this way, the lyrics are as nonedged as the music. Ride, for example, repeats short phrases almost like mantras, without specifically referring to a plot-line within each song. Just as My Bloody Valentine mixes vocals deep into each track so that they are less emphasized in each song's vocals-to-instruments proportions, the lyrics in many of these bands' work are anti-focused until, in some cases, they become more the sound of the words than their actual meaning. (Virtually every song by Slowdive illustrates this point.) The message becomes scattered, faded, blurred until it's unintelligible; or perhaps the message is that even if you could understand the words, they wouldn't mean or solve anything. In other words, they're miasma-ed out.

Ride lead singer Mark Gardener's vocal style is similar to that of other miasma bands like the Boo Radleys, Catherine Wheel, and

Chapterhouse: fey, nearly effeminate, and wispy. It's as if the vocals are so swept away by the sheer feedback force of the music that the only energy left for them is soft, un-spotlighted. Some people may see these almost girly vocals as some big politically correct statement about sexual equality – sort of the vocal analog of fans both male and female in long-sleeved t-shirts and Doc Marten boots. But I don't: Miasma bands, like all the bands in this book, change the proportions of a standard pop song; for the miasmics the concentration is on washed-out guitar borders, via feedback and volume. So, the emphasis is off the vocals: If they're soft, that's fine. And frankly, the way miasmic bands mix their recordings with vocals buried beneath layers of whirling guitars would waste more husky vocals, anyway.

For Curve, whose debut LP, *Doppelganger*, came out in 1992 following a slew of British EPs, pop and fuzz go hand in hand. The band mixes some of the intentionally disorienting repetitions and song structures of the Valentines with layers of grinded guitars and catchy, almost trite pop songs. While the focus in a band like the Valentines is off its female vocalist, emphasizing the band as a band as opposed to a central vocalist with a backing band, Curve is structured around lead vocalist Toni Halliday, equal parts seductive and menacing, equal parts Chrissie Hynde, Siouxsie Sioux, Diamanda Galas, and cock tease. Since there's something to latch on to so clearly – musically and visually – it's basically miasma-pop.

Halliday's unabashed sexuality contrasts with the attitude of many of miasma's fans and musicians. While not exactly vocally feminist, the focus of so much of this music, as I've discussed, is comfortably off sex and sexuality. Fans dress in the same baggy t-shirt and jeans uniform, female members simply chug away at their instruments, sans mini-skirts or girly clichés. Curve's Toni Halliday, on the other hand, uses her femininity as a weapon. Unlike, say, the women in My Bloody Valentine, she is deliberately sexy and sexual, and that goes from her breathy vocals to her sultry live performance. It's no coincidence that the band's U.S.-only compilation of their three pre-LP British EPs is titled *Pubic Fruit*. The year-end readers polls in England's *New Musical Express* and *Melody Maker* named her "Number One Object of Desire" and "Number One Babe of the Year," respectively. She does give off a feeling of power, but it's a sex-based power like Madonna's rather than an "I'm equal" Valentines power. That slightly more traditional role may explain why Curve is finding accessibility in America more immediately than the Valentines are.

Also pop-based is the band Catherine Wheel, which layers its catchy tunes, like "Black Metallic" and "I Want to Touch You," with lashings of guitars and a meek, almost whined, anti-voice. And while pop songs are traditionally bound into a three-minute format, Catherine Wheel stretches the boundary to five and six minutes, gaining momentum and intensity via too-assertive-to-ignore, almost hyperbolically intense guitars. And so by processing what could have been clean, sweet little pop tunes through sheets of guitars, the band rejects the expected parameters of the mainstream, blurring the borders between "pop" and "alternative." Although you may be left humming a chorus, you're likely to feel haunted, exorcised, cleansed, or shaken up as well.

The Catherine Wheel brings up the issue of the casual but nonetheless noteworthy literary allusions some of these bands make. The name "Catherine Wheel" refers to the spiked cog that was used in the attempt to murder the Christian martyr Catherine of Alexandria. The writer Jean Stafford and the choreographer Twyla Tharp both composed pieces in their own media under that title. Directly, it implies both heraldry and violence (which somewhat parallels the band's actual blend of pop and roar), but it also nods to the band's intelligence. After all, it's hardly a name like the Ronettes or the Drifters. One of the pop music conventions alternative bands negate is the cliché of rock 'n' roll musicians as dumb, or at least not exactly literary mavens. Getting into the specifics of the meanings of band names in detail would require a different book, but it's worth pointing out that if you assume that serious fans of alternative music become part of a larger social picture—wearing a certain kind of clothing, hanging out at specific places where other alternative fans hang out, watching certain kinds of movies—then alternative band names like Bauhaus (after the art movement), Gang of Four (after the Chinese revolutionaries), Pere Ubu (after the play *Ubu Roi*), Shelleyan Orphan (after the poet Percy Bysshe Shelley), and Cabaret Voltaire (after the art movement) indicate an informed, intelligent demographic.

Which leads, as long as you acknowledge their reference to their namesake character in *To Kill a Mockingbird*, to the Boo Radleys. Although they're often compared to My Bloody Valentine, Liverpool's Boo Radleys blend loads of other influences into their sound, which resonates with everything from Coltrane to flamenco to American grunge-sters like Dinosaur Jr. It's that mix that makes their debut album, *Everything's Alright Forever*, more long-term memorable than some of their contemporaries' releases. While it's easy to grasp the musical entirety of the work of bands like Curve and Catherine Wheel in one listen, the Boos' music still offers new nuances thirty listens in.

To shove the Boos (as their fans call them) to the front of the MBV-influenced pack is a heady claim. So here's the proof: It's not that they defy their influences—it would be impossible to hear tracks like "Does This Hurt?" and "Losing It (Song for Abigail)" from their Creation debut album, *Everything's Alright Forever* (which came out in the United States on Columbia), and not bring their whir down to the Valentines—but that they blend a variety of influences with a respect and complexity that is simply more elegant than most of the work of their contemporaries. If Curve is miasma pop, the Boos are jazzy-grungy-arty-revved-up miasma-rock. It may sound like a mishmash, but it gives their music real substance. Clear examples of this breadth of scope can be heard on *Everything's Alright Forever*'s first few commanding tracks, from the Miles Davis–influenced "Spaniard" to the cacophonous "Towards the Light" to the pop-based "Losing It (Song for Abigail)." Their EPs, several of which came out before the album did, all show leaps-and-bounds growth; but it is the jump on the *Boo! Forever* EP (available as a British import on Creation), from the Beach-Boys-meet-grunge tracks like "Boo! Forever" and "Buffalo Bill" to the house-beat-pulsed "Sunfly II: Walking with the Kings," that shows the depth of the band and how it's evolving. And with that evolution continuing to unfold—as you can hear on their sophisticated, dense *Lazarus* EP—it becomes even clearer that the Boos use the miasmic sound as a base to jump off of instead of as an end in itself.

This rundown of miasma bands shows their impact. It's not intended to be all-encompassingly comprehensive—it simply shows the impact a band like the Valentines have had and the way different individual musicians blend their own contributions with the miasma sound. It's worth noting that in addition to all the British bands listed above, American bands like Boston's Drop Nineteens and the Swirlies, Lancaster, Pennsylvania's Lilys, and Delaware's Smashing Orange also base their music around a miasmatic growl. It's the Brit-heavy playlists of American college radio stations that enabled those bands to hear groups like My Bloody Valentine that would influence them in the first place. Admittedly, however, the distance between

England and America delayed the onslaught of these U.S. counterparts until a couple of years after the British miasma bands got started. Nonetheless, the universality of emotions like confusion and despair makes miasma music resonate in America as loudly as it does in England.

Because there are less automatic components to grasp on to, miasma fans at gigs often aren't singing along with every word. How could they really understand every word? Except for the new school of young American male fans who seem to mosh to just about anything, the standard M.O. is standing near-still, head bobbing, intent but not too physical. It's as if too much motion would take the focus away from the music, which *live* is almost necessarily extremely loud — as if to intensify the big, beautiful fuzz of the music even more.

Paralleling the music is much of the album cover art these artists use. On My Bloody Valentine's *Loveless* and *Isn't Anything*, along with, to pull a few quick examples, Ride's *Nowhere*, Slowdive's *Just for a Day*, and Catherine Wheel's *Ferment*, blurry or hard-to-decipher pictures cover the albums. Without an easy image to latch on to, they are visual analogs to the music they contain. Many of these bands' videos are also steeped in that haze. But these miasma-ed components of a band's presentation of themselves to the public are not, at least in the case of these bands, part of some artificial, superimposed marketing plan. They often pick up elements of the band-generated stage show, as with My Bloody Valentine's blurry stage slides' being echoed by their album cover. Most major labels that distribute and license alternative bands are comfortable with this sort of integration because marketers know that in this world bands are similar to their fan base and so understand what they want, don't want, and expect.

The bottom line is that kids, by getting religious-fanatic-passionate about a band, find a group of friends and a wardrobe and a way to spend their time and long for escape, something to make them stand out and feel like they have a place. Miasma music offers that escape, but it's a false exit: The miasmic's place is as weird and complicated as the real world.

BRITISH THREE GUITAR BANDS

It may seem redundant to label a genre of bands "guitar bands"; after all, virtually every band mentioned in this book delivers its sound through a mass of guitars. But what I'm calling guitar bands differ from other bands in that they so clearly focus their sound around their guitars and what those instruments can do. It's as if, in an age of sampling and synths, these bands are consciously doing something purer, more musical, more closely linked with, say, Elvis Presley or the Beatles than with more immediate antecedents.

Some of these bands might be labeled "garage bands" by some fans or critics. That term has come to stand for an intentionally loose, warm, and raucous style of guitar music with heavy mid-sixties roots. But I believe "garage band" just isn't a valid way to describe the bulk of these bands. Although their influences, sounds, and fans can be clumped together, anything more specific than the common factor of a guitar base seems forced. And, certainly, bands like the Wedding Present or Kitchens of Distinction (which I'll concentrate on in this chapter) or Sonic Youth or Dinosaur Jr. (the focal points of Chapter 4) have more sophistication and complexity than your average rip-it-up garage band. You could call these groups "jangle bands" or "grunge bands," defining them by their style, which revolves around the strummed grit of loud electric guitars. But the bottom line is simply that these musicians center their sound around guitars and the no-bullshit use of those guitars, period.

Beyond that, guitar bands split, at least to my ears, between a British school and an American school in much the same way that punk circa 1977 had two factions: the angry, political British clan (exemplified by bands like the Sex Pistols and the Clash) and the sweeter, CBGB school of the Ramones and Blondie. There are, of course, crossovers; this is exemplified by New York–based Television, whose seminal album, *Marquee Moon* (1977), hugely influenced alternative bands on both sides of the Atlantic. But, for the most part, the two countries' guitar bands sound different, express similar musical intentions differently, and attract fans who dress differently and dance differently. And although there are, say, loads of British fans of New York–based Sonic Youth and many Americans who love the Wedding Present, distinctions affected by the artists' surroundings and the inspiration they provide still codify musical movements.

Furthermore, British guitar bands like the Fall and the Wedding Present – and, conversely, American ones like Sonic Youth and Dinosaur Jr. – embody the ethic, stance, and look of their surroundings with the inevitable authenticity of a used fifties high school letter jacket or, to pull a more recent example, a Public Enemy t-shirt. For a British kid to be into Nirvana or an American kid to be into the Chameleons is about more than music – it's as much a cultural exchange as the German chancellor feeding the American president local beer and wurst. To opt for an alternative band, and that band's grimy t-shirt or ripped jeans or liberal politics, is to choose a specific cultural exchange. Alternative music fans elect the England of the John Peel show and the Fall instead of Masterpiece Theatre and George Michael; their British counterparts choose Sonic Youth's depressed, neo-apocalyptic vision of urban America over the synthetic gleam of *The Cosby Show*. In that way, the distinction between the British and American schools of guitar bands is drawn even more severely, independent of which side of the Atlantic their fans are on.

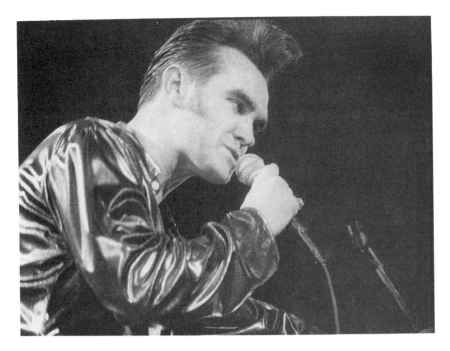

The Smiths' Morrissey

The roots of much of the edged-out guitar sound that is integral to British guitar bands like the Wedding Present and Kitchens of Distinction can be heard in two bands. One is British and one is American, respectively: Wire and Television. On early albums like *Pink Flag* (its 1977 debut) and *Chairs Missing* (its follow-up the next year), Wire uses tight, clipped guitars to express the frustration of punk through an almost antagonistic jangle instead of yelp-it-out fury—the resulting music still vents all that rage and is equally compelling. As is clear from tracks like "Ex Lion Tamer," "Feeling Called Love," and "A Question of Degree," those juggernaut guitars are paced behind a decidedly average, British-accented, almost spoken singing voice, raspy and pretentionless and oh-so-normal. The combination—which is at the core of the sound of the Fall and the Wedding Present—is like an afternoon cup of tea with a razor blade in its saucer.

Television—featuring the gorgeous, distinctive guitar of Richard Lloyd and the poetic strain of the stage-named Tom Verlaine (after Romantic poet Paul Verlaine)—uses a similar formula of pop songs topped with the Woody Allen-esque neurosis of quivering guitars. Although the band re-formed in the early nineties to release a self-titled comeback album in 1992, the band's real impact came in its first incarnation with its debut LP, *Marquee Moon*. The group shone with stripped-down but emphatic guitars; and although its base was downtown New York, its distinctive ringing, edgy sound (best heard on *Marquee Moon*'s title track) resonates in the music of bands like the Fall and the Wedding Present. Television has also influenced a slew of bands — like the Feelies and Mission of Burma — who in turn influenced their own musical descendants who are equally compelled by their uptight jangle of wired-out guitars.

There are more immediate precursors to the music of Kitchens of Distinction and the Wedding Present as well: the Smiths, the Fall, and the vastly under-credited Chameleons — three guitar bands with guts, theatricality, and an almost archaic elegance. Led by Morrissey (born Steven Patrick Morrissey, but going professionally simply by his surname), a dynamic, camp, nearly crooning vocalist with an El-vised quiff hairdo and a taunting, provocative style, the Smiths exploded in England in late 1983 and early 1984. They offered listeners a no-bullshit alternative to a chart filled with the lowest-common-denominator synth-pop of Howard Jones and Nik Kershaw. The Smiths' music was the antithesis of the top-40 of the time and provided the same no-frills release that punk did from an equally bland mid-seventies musical climate. But to peg Morrissey as the key to the Smiths is to miss the point: The backbone of the band was lead guitarist Johnny Marr, whose urgent, slightly rockabilly jangle propelled not only his band but, indirectly, a whole slew of bands who copped his seductive, sauntering style.

Yet Morrissey's stage presence — larger than life but rooted in real-person reality — is unavoidable; his "starness" — from his bounding across the stage to his always-recognizable vocals to his press rantings for vegetarianism, celibacy, and Oscar Wilde — focused his band in a way, say, none of the miasma bands are. Although, as I just pointed out, the band was musically contingent on the sum of its parts, Morrissey as center of (at least visual) attraction is echoed by the Wedding Present's David Gedge and others. And although there is an almost tangible darkness to what the Smiths do, Morrissey graced its music with more than a touch of glamour.

In the specific case of Morrissey, who has gone on to a successful solo career (particularly in America, where heavy airplay on commercial alternative radio stations — which play the most accessible end of the typical college station's playlist, plus commercials — has made him a big concert draw), glamour and camp go hand in hand. The singer's flamboyance on stage—prancing around with handfuls of flowers (with the Smiths) or a bare chest (in his solo shows)—brings to mind the hyper-drama of a drag show; nevertheless, he never states his sexual preference outright. To me, and to so many alternative fans, formal issues of gender and sexual preference seem a touch removed, and almost anti-relevant, to the music. There is a recognizable sexuality to the music and image of an artist like Morrissey, but whether he's straight, gay, bisexual, or even, as he claims, celibate, makes no difference—as long as the music's good. The generation of fans and performers who make up the alternative realm are hip to gay rights; they've dealt with issues like AIDS and abortion rights for the past decade. So unless an artist declares his or her sexual preference (and even then, with openly gay artists like Phranc and Kitchens of Distinction lead singer Patrick Fitzgerald, it's about honesty as opposed to shock value), playful (or not so playful) ambiguity is easily accepted.

That acceptance reiterates the fact that the world of alternative music is a specific demographic. Alternative fans share coherent tastes and beliefs: Morrissey fans (and fans of the other bands discussed in this book) aren't put off by something that might seem out of the ordinary in everyday life, like men with multi-pierced ears or with lipstick. Performers like Morrissey, along with former-Eurythmic Annie Lennox and lead singer Brett Anderson from the British band Suede, blur the barriers between what is traditionally male or female in the same way that the miasmics blur the edges of their songs. Morrissey's on-stage theatrics, Lennox's early look of short hair and men's suits, and Anderson's feminine hair and pouty lips don't raise an eyebrow in the alternative world. These artists' twisting of sexual roles parallels Dinosaur Jr.'s sonic roar or My Bloody Valentine's haze—that is, they twist the audience's expectations. For a group of fans that includes women in clunky men's Doc Marten boots and pierced-eared men, those twists seem totally natural.

It would be careless while addressing the twisting of sexual roles to ignore its direct musical antecedents: the glam rockers of the seventies like T. Rex, David Bowie, and the New York Dolls. For these performers, traditionally female stage elements like lipstick and high heels became integral parts of their shows; the point was to be noticed and have fun. There is also a definite nonspecificity of gender addressed on an album like David Bowie's *Ziggy Stardust and the Spiders from Mars*. Of course, glam rockers embodied a kind of escapism, and the alternative bands of the late eighties and early nineties are rooted in the real: the Smiths, Kitchens of Distinction, and the Wedding Present all sing about issues that affect and so involve their listeners. Yet there's an almost tangible grandness in much of Morrissey's work; from the use of homosexual slang in "Piccadilly Palare" (from the 1990 *Bona Drag* collection) to the loaded visual images in his video of pretty quiffed boys following him around ("We Hate It when Our Friends Become Successful") to footage of little boys dressing up in women's clothing in the video for "Interesting Drug." The theatricality of Morrissey or Brett Anderson (the frontman for the band Suede) is over the top and almost out of control. But it does send out the message to fans that it's okay to be bold and wild and not conform with standard definitions of "appropriate behavior."

Admittedly much of the Smiths' impact has to do with their meaty sound—equal parts Buzzcocks, Elvis, the moaning voice of loneliness, and their own unique jumble of other influences and original devices, yet it's impossible to discuss the band's influence (and importance in the bigger picture) without examining its lyrics. First of all, Morrissey's lyrics are sophisticated and literary in a way that pop music traditionally isn't (which fulfills one of the conditions that Jameson attributes to postmodernism, that there be no break between high and low art, as in the lyrics of bands like the Clash, not to mention everything from Jeff Koons's photography to Mark Morris's choreography). The Smiths' song "Cemetery Gates" mentions Keats and Yeats; the album titles of *The Queen Is Dead* and *Louder than Bombs* are taken, respectively, from Hubert Selby, Jr.'s, *Last Exit to Brooklyn* and Elizabeth Smart's *By Grand Central Station I Sat Down and Wept*. Hardly boy-meets-girl stories, Morrissey's Smiths-era lyrics bring up issues like sexual perversity and desire ("Well I Wonder"), vegetarianism ("Meat Is Murder"), and the deranged morals of the so-called Moors Murderers, who killed a slew of young children in northern England ("Suffer Little Children"). Most prevalent are recurrent allusions to feelings of inadequacy, loneliness, insecurity, and an obsession with death.

Those last concerns make a major point: If adolescence is a period in people's lives when they feel like outsiders—like they are not beautiful or clever or cool enough—then Morrissey's lyrics are the embodiment of adolescence. Just as the teenage boy's bedroom is a haven for that bundle of insecure feelings, the Smiths' music is a musical bedroom where those feelings of gloomy outsider-ness can be expressed, yelled about, even extolled.

The Smiths' articulation of the emotional Sturm und Drang of adolescence is as present in the band's Morrissey-written lyrics as in its music. Morrissey's lyrics touch people in the exact same way that Sylvia Plath's poems or Egon Schiele's paintings do—by articulating an experience as if to say "It's okay, I've gone through this too, let's suffer together." Yet Morrissey's lyrics whimper with a gloom usually reserved for a suicide note. Even a single line can show the depression: "I am human and I need to be loved," he implores in the cut "How Soon Is Now?" Or, to pull a couplet from the song "Half a Person": "Sixteen, clumsy, and shy/That's the story of my life." For other bands, sheer volume and intensity is the articulation of pain. Everyone from Sonic Youth to Black Sabbath employs this technique. For the Smiths, however, with song titles like "Heaven Knows I'm Miserable Now," "Unlovable," "Never Had No One Ever," and "Panic," alienation is expressed lyrically.

The other key component of the Smiths' music that has influenced many other guitar bands is its sheer Britishness. Certainly, there are a myriad of lyrical references to British life, from the scene of an overdisciplined boys' school in "The Headmaster Ritual" to the self-explanatory "The Queen Is Dead." The band's Anglocentrism goes further than that, however. There is this grim, stiff-upper-lipped jangle to its music that is somehow almost inexplicably British. It's the aural equivalent of a cup of tea on a dank, inclement day or fish and chips dripping with malt vinegar wrapped in flat absorbent paper. If that sounds forced, then try this analogy: The Smiths' sound parallels the gritty, realist, anti-Hollywood British films of the late fifties and early sixties, like *A Taste of Honey* and *Room at the Top*, in their expression of the the dark brown realities of British, particularly northern British, life. It's no coincidence that the stars of those films, like Terrence Stamp and *A Taste of Honey*'s Rita Tushingham, adorn the Smiths' album and singles covers. Their association with the no-frills dynamics of British working-class life perfectly illustrates the music underneath their images.

That the Smiths express their northern British backgrounds is an important concept for several reasons. The Smiths are from Manchester, England's second-largest city and the cultural center of England's north. In the seventies, as punk was happening, London had bands like the Clash and the Sex Pistols. But Manchester had the Buzzcocks: four balls of revved-up, almost spastic energy who ripped through popped-out tunes and expressed a lot of personal frustration. A few simple titles, like "What Do I Get," "Orgasm Addict," and "I Don't Know What to Do with My Life" give a sense of what they're about lyrically: the intensity, bite, and special mix of big-city urbanism with warm, homey provincialism that typifies Manchester and its people. The Buzzcocks were (and still are) hugely influential to a number of bands. They certainly were to the Smiths.

Manchester in the past fifteen to twenty years has been much affected by England's political and financial climate—from mid-seventies unemployment to late eighties/early nineties recession. Certainly, many cities have been forced to deal with unemployment and hard times, but somehow kids from Manchester (like kids from Akron, Ohio, or Seattle, Washington, or even circa-Supremes Detroit) have been able, and have probably needed, to transfer the depression of their surroundings into music. The Mancunian need for musical and sensory escape bred bands like the Stone Roses and the Charlatans in the late eighties and early nineties. The music of these bands was part of a larger partied attitude focused around clubbing and, for many kids, taking the drug Ecstasy.

But it's more than that: Just as certain bands somehow breathe the life of their surroundings into their music (the Red Hot Chili Peppers just feel like L.A.; vintage Ramones records sound like the soundtrack to downtown New York), there is in most of these bands a common, amorphic, notable mark of cold, rainy, depressed northern England. That imprint may not be distinctly pinpointable, but it's unquestionably there. It runs through bands like New Order, which was started from the remnants of the very depressed Joy Division, whose morose elegance was an influence on many bands. And the mark runs through the Smiths and through even poppier bands like the Inspiral Carpets. It also runs through the key bands mentioned in this chapter: the Chameleons and the Wedding Present (both from nearby Leeds), Kitchens of Distinction (featuring Mancunian lead singer Patrick Fitzgerald), and the Fall.

To focus on the Fall is to focus on Mark E. Smith, who, to an American raised on hyperbolic superstars (take your pick: Elvis Presley, Michael Jackson, and now Madonna), probably seems the world's most unlikely frontman. Weedy, plain, in humble, Joe Aver-

Mark E. Smith from the Fall

age clothes, workingman's pint in his hand, Smith is everyman, an antihero, and that's a huge element of his appeal. In that way, to a whole generation of British indie fans the success of the Fall is similar, on a smaller scale, to Nirvana's huge success—its no-bullshit, intense, "I'm-one-of-you" music. On albums from *Perverted by Language* to *The Frenz Experiment* to more recent albums like *Extricate,* that common denominator of accessibility—in a "stancical" way as opposed to a "stick-in-your-head-pop-song" way—is always present.

And to focus on the Fall is also to focus on Mark Smith's voice, a near-spoken, angsty, sometimes whiny hybrid somewhere between late-sixties Lou Reed circa "I'm Waiting for the Man" and "White Light, White Heat," Bob Dylan, and a working-class version of Oscar Wilde. Obviously, the immediate lack of polish of his vocals has a lot to do with the accessibility I'm getting at. The Fall has also influenced a whole slew of bands, most relevantly (and intensely) the Wedding Present and Kitchens of Distinction, but also the Blue Aeroplanes, American bands like Pavement, and loads of others. To have a lead singer with such a nonsinger's voice is to let fans know that "it's okay, you don't have to be professional, you can do this too." It's the same call to arms as the Sex Pistols'; it's the same appeal as Nirvana's; it's the same antidote to manufactured MTV. And it's that encouragement to kids that there is some reality and bite left to music, that it doesn't have to be New Kids on the Block or Paula Abdul, produced and glitzed out and sweetened with contrivance—and *this* is the key to the appeal of the entire realm of alternative music.

It's also the links that alternative music has to reactionary movements from Situationism to Dadaism to postmodernism that make it appealing. Alternative music contradicts the unaffecting norms of mainstream music in the same way that those movements in the visual arts contradict representational, "conventional" art. To put it another way, the Fall is to, say, Milli Vanilli as the work of anyone from Man Ray to Marcel Duchamp to postmodern painter Julian Schnabel is to the *Mona Lisa*. That link—which Greil Marcus studies through punk in his meaty *Lipstick Traces*—can also be seen in the way the movements of modern dance compare with those of classic ballet, the clash of the gutsy theater of John Osborne and Harold Pinter with, to draw an extreme example, the plays of William Shakespeare, and the contrast between the simplicity of films by Francois Truffaut and Jean-Luc Godard and films produced in Hollywood. The point is that young people—and not-so-young people—need art that speaks to them, that represents their views, that they can relate to. And if the arts of a certain era can't fulfill that basic need, countermovements arise that can. And so Roy Lichtenstein and Andy Warhol rejected the norms of said art with their vibrant pop culture–based pop art, Pedro Almodovar has been speaking to post-Franco Spanish youth through his wild, anti-censored films, and alternative bands discard the norms of mainstream artists like, say, John Cougar Mellencamp to create music that resonates with a specific group of listeners. And so, for pretentionless-real people, the Fall's Mark E. Smith is an anti-star, an anti-hero, an anti-icon.

Mark E. Smith's "everyman-ness" goes further than based-in-Manchester provincialism: His vocals and the Fall's music are built around the same subconscious but ever-present Anglocentrism of the Smiths. It is tough to articulate without sounding terribly contrived, but Fall records, just like Smiths records and Jam records and even early Beatles and Who records, just sound British (and not just because the voices have British accents). It's the equivalent of the Eagles' "Hotel California" or Linda Ronstadt's "Hurt So Bad" reeking of mid-seventies California-ness. The British tone is a key to why the Fall appeals to British indie kids and perhaps helps to explain why the band, like the Jam and the Buzzcocks before them, has never been a big seller in America. In the band's native England, a country dominated by American television shows and movies and Coca-Cola and Big Macs and Levi's jeans, the very British Fall is not only everyman but the local everyman, a band that one can relate to because its members could live next door. Certainly, the Fall is not the only British band to have that appeal – the Clash did scream "I'm So Bored with the U.S.A" in 1977. Nevertheless, the Fall exemplifies a certain stance. Furthermore, ranting in his northern accent, Smith tells the Fall's fans, without necessarily needing to spell it out, that one doesn't need to come from America to be a rock star. Hey, in Smith's view, a rock star doesn't even need to come from England's affluent capital of London. As Smith himself declares in the song "Totally Wired," "You don't have to be an American brand."

But it's not just that the Fall reeks of England; the band reeks of an England filled with unemployment, racism, and the harshness of northern towns like Manchester, Middlesbrough, Hull, Newcastle-Upon-Tyne. It's not that the Fall necessarily addresses these issues in lyrics (although they often do, as in "Cash and Carry"'s discussion of Manchester's supermarkets and factories and a local independent record label, Factory), it's that the denied anger in Smith's voice, the abrasion of the guitars, and the punch of the drums comes directly from the frustration of coping with depressing social conditions day in and day out. It's a different anger than the one that underlies the music of, say, Sonic Youth or Nirvana. It's a product of life on the dole (England's welfare system) paired with Queen Elizabeth on the television and marmite on toast for breakfast. As often as British issues are addressed in the band's lyrics, the Fall's Anglocentrism is understood and felt rather than pinpointed. For proof, you can check out the vocals on the debut album by the American band Pavement, *Slanted and Enchanted*. Although they are completely derived from Mark E. Smith's, they have an entirely different feel. Early releases by Washington, D.C.'s, Unrest—like "Can't Sit Still" on its 1988 *Malcolm X Park* LP—equally reek of the Fall's influence, but have an inherently different feel. Smith's lyrics are centered around their surroundings as firmly as trademark Joan Didion novels or David Hockney swimming pool paintings are based in southern California, or a sixties Godard film is based in Paris.

Regionalism has been the cogs of the alternative machine, namely, bands, college radio stations, clubs, and small record shops. These localized parts of the alternative system allow bands to have core "fan bases," upon which they can build for more widespread success. Pulling away from the traditional (and limited) centers of music and the music industry—specifically, New York, Los Angeles, and London—alternative bands, labels, and stores speak to "real" people, without urban slickness. Many of the centers of alternative music are in towns and small cities: Chapel Hill, North Carolina (home of the Merge label, which is run by the band Superchunk); Athens, Georgia (which spawned mega-successes like R.E.M. and the B-52's); Liverpool, England (the base of the Zoo label in the early eighties, with bands like the Teardrop Explodes and Echo and the Bunnymen); Bristol, England (the base of Sarah Records, which releases bands like Heavenly and the Sweetest Ache); and Washington, D.C. (where a group of band-run indies like Dischord, Teen-Beat, and Simple Machines, owned by and featuring, respectively, Fugazi, Unrest, and Tsunami, are located). And there's even Seattle, where SubPop, the original home of Nirvana, operates. In all these places, bands, label owners, and fans have rejected the big-budget status quo of major-label music and attitudes and used their own resources to produce something a lot more personal in a grass-roots way.

For the bands, this personal touch is not necessarily an issue of lyrics. The point of these regional scenes is that they allow a teenage kid in, say, D.C. to relate to a band whose members dress like he does and hang out at the same stores he does, that decorates its album sleeves the way he would, and that performs at a club where he can stand close enough to see them and maybe even talk to them afterward. Alternative bands—at least the ones in this book—are about reality. There're no frills but no bullshit either. Alternative bands are accessible to their fans in a way that superstars just aren't. In a world (musical and otherwise) of surface and fabrication, alternative music is about the empathized bond between performer and fan.

According to the indie/alternative ethic, the point is to reach not for the common denominator that will appeal to the most people (as Whitney Houston or George Michael do, for example) but to express just what you feel in your world, opting for a specific, personal center over an accepted mega-city like L.A. or London. Compare this urge to, say, that of Italian neorealist filmmaker Vittorio deSica or British Liverpudlian poets like Adrian Henri and Roger McGeogh—the impulse expresses what's close to home in a form that is appropriate to that home. Of course, these regional scenes have a sociological significance as well as a musical one. A band from North Carolina like Superchunk just sounds right next to local bands like Finger or Polvo; Nirvana makes a good double bill with lesser-known Seattle natives the Melvins and Mudhoney. One region's bands express the feelings, dress, and attitude of that region in a way that another region's bands just can't. To return to Manchester, bands like the Fall express the sentiments of their neighbors—whether lyrically or simply with a sound that just sounds right there, or clothes that look appropriate there, or even just an accent that feels comfortable and identifiable there.

The Fall's musical influence on other guitar bands is more direct as well. Backing Smith's monologued growl is an insurgent, chunky guitar line and an often almost awkward beat—there's something slightly off-kilter, nearly discordant, usually disconcerting about the band's sound. That scratch-that-itch guitar, often played by Craig Gannon (who played with the Smiths before their demise), is like bathroom sink drip. It's steady and ever so slightly abrasive, but after it gets going, it's hard to imagine it being turned off. If the common goal of the alternative bands is to take expected, "normal" music and twist it out of shape, bend it to make it theirs, then the Fall's blend of too-enunciated, too-spoken—mixed too high, running a different race than the music they front—embodies that goal.

But it's important not to ignore Smith's lyrics, which are as fragmented and intentionally obtuse as a novel by Louis Ferdinand Celine. Using snippets of imagery to draw an overall picture, Smith's lyrics are the antithesis of, say, "Baby, I Love You." They're choppy and cryptic and revel in average, everyday life, as is shown in songs like "Rollin' Dany," "Hit the North," and "Cash and Carry." They are unpretentious; they're often bitingly cynical takes on modern Manchester life – and just about anything else that strikes Smith's fancy. They sometimes include almost Balzacian specific, image-capturing details – everyday actions like walking down the street, going to the pub. Often they are broken into stanzas, but just as often they're prose-based rants, as is shown in the following line from "New Face In Hell": "A prickly line of sweat covers enthusiast's forehead as the realisation [*sic*] hits him that the same government him and his now dead neighbour voted for and backed and talked of on cream porches have tricked him into their war against the people who enthusiast and dead hunter would have wished torture on." It's not hard to see that if the pop establishment is George Michael singing "I want your sex," Mark E. Smith is not just inherently alternative – he's practically a rock 'n' roll poet laureate.

It can certainly be argued that other, nonalternative artists – like, say, Bob Dylan – write lyrics that are more poetry than singsong, half-assed musical accompaniment; and of course, that's true. It's just that Smith's lyrics scan like poetry; songs like "Totally Wired," "Eat Y'self Fitter," "Oswald Defence Lawyer," and endless others are like tightly mapped-out poetic verse. To cite a quick example, "Ladybird (Green Grass)," off 1993's *The Infotainment Scam*, features the lines: "And there's a big concert going down in this town/People can see society broken down/I said up on the green grass but it just brought me down/And the words that get up and it just brought me round." In addition, the lines are not only delivered in an orator's near-spoken voice but backed (unlike an early-sixties Dylan, with an anti-emphasized acoustic guitar) with music that is totally in sync with them rhythmically. Like a twentieth-century counterpoint to an ancient Greek chorus, this rhythm and substantial lyric go hand in hand. And for the Fall, the rhythm is more jolted, jagged, and raucous than you'd expect; its accompanying lyrics are more weighty than they are "supposed to be." The band's music combines the biting commentary that previously was the territory of folk songs, newspaper headlines, or political commentary with gnarly guitars. Certainly, the blending of lyrical substance and musical bite is part of what the Clash, the Sex Pistols, Sonic Youth, and many other bands do—but the way the Fall mixes the two is all its own.

There's an added twist with the Fall's lyrics: They are like a painting or poem with intentionally obtuse imagery; you can usually decipher only snippets/half-lines/chunks here and there. While not exactly art for art's sake, the combination of design and deliverance gives Smith's performed lyrics an unattainable quality—they are mysterious because you just can't understand them all. This elusiveness seems somehow incredibly appropriate combined with edgy music propelled by an even edgier leader. It reminds me of the paintings of Jean Michel Basquiat: You can make out some of the allusions, some of the references, chunks of allusions, but it's the effort of deciphering it—and, as strange as it may sound, never quite getting all of it—which is half the fun.

In addition, the Fall's lyrics certainly express the prevalent alternative notion that rock lyrics needn't be disposable and singsong; on the contrary, just as everyday language and subjects in the poetry of someone like Philip Larkin break the boundaries between high art and low art, lyrics as poetry break a similar boundary between traditional pop lyrics—lightweight, singalong boy-meets-girl tales—and lyrics with a real, substantial message, expressed in an intelligent, literary way. Even just a couple of lines show this intelligence; take, for example, a chunk of the song "C.R.E.E.P.": "Black saucers at the back of your neck/Interruptions, from the side when you talk is offending, make sure you're not absorbed." Equally heavy—and out of the usual pop music mode—is "Totally Wired"'s image of "A butterfly stomach round ground." Clearly, Smith's sometimes prosaic, often literary, equal-parts-mystery-and-venom lyrics certainly break that preconception of rock lyrics as trite, clichéd, and vacuous.

The Fall's desire for a literary identity is obvious too from the lyrics' frequent allusions to literature and the other arts: One album, *Bend Sinister*, borrows its title from a Nabokov novel; one song is called "Doctor Faustus," nodding at the Thomas Mann novel; and the band sets to music—arguably demolishing—William's Blake's "Jerusalem." A Fall song—"Hey! Luciani"—was expanded into a play; a Fall album, "I Am Curious Oranj," a nod to its dubious decedents, was the soundtrack to a dance piece by avant-garde choreographer Michael Clark.

A key influence on the Fall is a band called the Chameleons, who likewise root their music in the gloomy north of England. That band's moody, dark, layered guitar sound serves as a direct precursor for bands like the Wedding Present and Kitchens of Distinction. Big and cavernous, the Chameleons' music is equal parts sleazy club and majestic cathedral—it's magnificent, expansive, elegant but gutsy guitar music. If the surging, raw energy of punk went to charm school, listening to heavy doses of early Genesis records, it would probably sound like the Chameleons.

But the Chameleons' (who had to be called "The Chameleons U.K." in America for legal reasons) sound is not just about grandness. The music is juxtaposed against another almost anti-voice: the strain of lead singer/bassist Mark Burgess. Combined with relentless drums and lyrics addressing sadness, desperation ("I'm running a race, I've got to keep going"), and feelings of inadequacy (some song titles: "Things I Wish I'd Said," "Soul in Isolation," "P.S. Goodbye"), that voice urgently pulls the listener in. Even the band's album titles, like *What Does Anything Mean? Basically?* and *Strange Times*, capture the feelings of doom and helplessness that permeate many of the band's lyrics.

Of course, this exploration of gloom is Morrissey territory, Sylvia Plath territory, Rainer Werner Fassbinder territory—the unsure turf that is so identifiable to an insecured-out teenager. But the Chameleons' impact is not primarily a lyrical one; it's the band's equally insistent and imposing sound which leads a direct line to the bands I'll concentrate on in the rest of this chapter: Kitchens of Distinction and the Wedding Present. For me, the Chameleons' key message is that it's okay for music to be beautiful and frenzied at once—that it can still express all those cool angsty feelings without spike. This combination of morose attitude and stance but almost chillingly lovely, glorious songs is probably clearest on *Strange Times*, which was released in 1986. In many ways, that album best fulfills the band's beauty-with-bite musical goals. On its tracks like "In Answer" and "Time," guitars surround the listener, transposing the listening environment, demanding to be heard. Equally insistent—and here's where a lot of the influence lies—is Burgess's voice, almost yelling but never quite needing to, not exactly hitting the notes without it ever mattering, singing aggressively, passionately, in a style that brings to mind the spoken word over a trained singer's. In other words, Burgess is another everyman.

Following in this dark tradition are Kitchens of Distinction, three normal, overeducated-by-rock-and-roll-standards, powerful players.

Kitchens of Distinction

From its first album, *Love Is Hell* (which was released here by Rough Trade in 1990), to its most recent and third release, *The Death of Cool* (A&M), the band combines the kind of larger-than-life beauty of the Chameleons, the gritty, dangerously-near-spoken vocals of the Fall, and the theatricality of the Smiths with a spacy, whooshy guitar sound (courtesy of lead guitarist Julian Swales). The mix brings to mind everything from a sound effects record to a room full of synthesizers. The salient guitar sound that sets the band apart from the others discussed in this chapter comes from delay pedals attached to Swales's single guitar – up to eight of them – which allow the band to somehow sound like a compact punchy trio and a large expansive group at the same time. If the Kitchens' music was a poem, it would be Paul Verlaine's "Epilogue" or Charles Baudelaire's "Elevation" or "Exotic Perfume" from *Les Fleurs du Mal*. Romantic, flowery, almost regal, the sound bursts out emphatically like a speeded-up 16mm film of a flower in mid-bloom.

If we accept the notion that alternative music, by (this book's) definition, twists expected musical norms, then that large, enveloping sound is the alternative take on Phil Spector's famous "wall of sound." More specifically, Kitchens take the expansive sound that became Spector's trademark and contort it into something less optimistic, more moody, and pulsed by the chunky influence of punk. It's sort of Spector mixed with 1977 punk mixed with *Wuthering Heights*, stuck somewhere in Manchester. If the basis for the rock and pop mainstream is the catchy, love-song ditties of fifties and sixties top-40 radio, then a band like Kitchens — with expansive guitars, sophisticated lyrics written with (and requiring from the listener) thought and intelligence, and "Joe Average" vocals — is, by definition, alternative. As are, for that matter, bands that use a similar formula, like the Fall and the Smiths (even though the end results sound different). And I would argue that this definition of alternative is interchangeable, in the context of these bands, with the term "postmodern": Acknowledging past rock structures and systems, keeping the ones that work (like catchy melodies and structures) and chucking the ones that don't, using devices that were formerly saved for "fine art," like published literature and the theater — that's postmodernism in action, and it's also the true spirit of alternative music.

That Kitchens sound has influenced a slew of the same bands that My Bloody Valentine has influenced: Lush, Ride, Moose, and so on. Somehow, however, Kitchens rarely gets credit for that impact. In England, they've never been trendy or the critics' darlings, and while influential British DJ John Peel, whose widely heard radio show is the main outlet for independent music in Great Britain, championed the Fall, the Smiths, the Wedding Present, and the Chameleons, only with their third album were Kitchens offered a prestigious session on his show. In contrast, in America, Kitchens' first major-label release, 1991's *Strange Free World*, topped the college radio charts and sold more than 60,000 copies — on alternative radio, in small clubs, on MTV's alternative music program, and in magazines like *Alternative Press*, they've had definite impact.

There's no easy explanation for this split between Kitchens' success abroad and in their native England. Some observers might cite the band's lack of a clear-cut image or a flashy lead singer, since other huge-in-England bands like the Fall and the Smiths feature both. Another reason might be that lead singer Patrick Fitzgerald's open homosexuality might turn some fans away, although I don't buy this one, myself, because sexual preference isn't usually an issue in the alternative world and, frankly, the band deemphasizes his open gayness — it's become just one of his attributes, like having red hair or a fondness for beer. If anything, the band's acceptance of its one gay member is no different from accepting any other quality or trait — it's beyond political correctness. Although it may be difficult to understand Kitchens' comparative lack of success in England, it is easy to see why American college and so-called commercial alternative stations (the handful of commercial stations, like WDRE in New York and KROQ in Los Angeles, which have playlists similar to a college station's) have embraced the group: There's something incredibly moving about its music. Kitchens of Distinction mixes cup-of-tea Englishness with an almost reggaeish bass-line (but, hey, that's just what the Clash did). The songs tell stories of lovers' fights and feelings of inadequacy and loneliness but are written just obtusely enough to be near-poems (yeah, but that's Smiths turf). And then they douse those lyrics and melodies in a whir of what seems like thirty guitars. Yet what you see and what is really there is this one little guy bouncing around like a raindrop dropping down into a puddle and gurgling back to the surface again and again on a big wide stage. Even if you're merely hearing it through headphones, it's just an aural feast.

As with the Smiths, the band writes lyrics that create a literary, rather than a bubble-gum, medium. Sure, many of their songs are about relationships and their evolution, but the approach to those relationships could be part of a Booker Prize novel. *Death of Cool*'s "Blue Pedal" describes life as "soft believing melted butter." "These Drinkers" (off the *Strange Free World* album) describes the moon as "a god with ideas of mirth." There are skewed references to literature: One of *Death of Cool*'s tracks is called "On Tooting Broadway Station," again an allusion to Elizabeth Smart's *By Grand Central Station I Sat Down and Wept*. The track's final chorus moans "My John of Arc," and so the band personalizes, resexes, mutates the Joan of Arc legend. It's an allusion without bowing. Thus, the band learns from its influences but synthesizes them for itself and its fans. To be taken in, the band's music, no matter how captivating it is live, requires a lot of listens.

The layered complexity that makes the band's music require so many listens may also explain the problem some potential fans have had with Kitchens. In a sense, it's a lot easier to be into a band like, say, Nirvana, than to be into Kitchens: The first time you hear a Nirvana song, you get the whole picture. Because of Kitchens' effulgent sound, kids aren't compelled to mosh or slam or get as physically attached to the music as they are with other bands. In fact, there is a sense of refinement to Kitchens music that doesn't attract kids so much as adults. That acceptance by "adults" – who may really be only a few years older than the group that would easily be called "kids" – provides a key distinction between the fans of bands like Nirvana and those of Kitchens. Adults don't get visibly "religious" about their bands; they have jobs and full lives, so the chances of their having blue hair or a pierced nose because their favorite rock star does is pretty slim. An adult isn't going to follow a band's tour around, paint the band's name on the back of a motorcycle jacket, or wait at the front of a stage for hours to grab the set list off the stage at the end of a gig. In my view, the terms "adult" and "kid" are more attitude than age: There can be sixteen-year-old adults and forty-year-old kids. And the band members of Kitchens, all thirty-ish, all three with university degrees and sophisticated musical tastes, attract adults as opposed to kids. And so, with all the repercussion it entails, they're no Nirvana.

The Wedding Present, in contrast, has attracted die-hard, intense fans, at least in England. From Leeds, the band shares many features with the other bands mentioned in this chapter: near-spoken, strained-at-the-top-of-the-throat vocals (very Fall-like), lyrics of failed relationships, an ever-present Anglocentric feel. Lead singer David Gedge's yelp – deep and guttural, gnawing from his throat as if he's going to scream in agony – is in-your-face intense and, to a traditional ear, antimusical. Again, the vocals exemplify the everyman ethic. Screaming about his lover who's cheated or doesn't care or has just left him, he's a soul singer in the purest sense. And, as the band's screaming guitars are, well, pounding in unison, they seem to drive the intensity home.

It's not a music that benefits from overanalysis. Its power comes from its no-holds-barred intensity. Virtually all the band's songs – from early singles like "My Favorite Dress" to more recent work – speed along with the force and determination of a purse thief blasting down the street with a freshly snatched handbag. To an audience of people repressing resentment against boss, teacher, shitty job, relationship-gone-sour, the "Weddoes" (as the British press calls them) are a cleansing screaming match, a therapy session. By chugging away at its guitars, lashing out at the drums, and growling into the microphone, the band vents its audience's variety of frustrations. Musically, what makes the Wedding Present really stand out is its mile-a-minute revved-up guitar, equal parts Velvet Underground and speed freak. If a migraine headache felt good, this is what it would feel like: throbbing, relentless, unavoidable.

Basically, those can't-shut-up guitars are the instrumental version of Gedge's vocals. There are loads of examples of this formula of booming vocals and guitars. To pick a couple: "Anyone Can Make a Mistake" (from the *George Best* LP, which is available only as an import in America); the spastic, shaky song "Brassneck" from *Bizarro*; "Suck" and "Dare" from the *Sea Monsters* LP. Because kids (as opposed to adults) can slam their heads up and down to the music's intense guitar buzz, its cathartic volume, and frontman David Gedge's easy-to-grasp-on-to growl, the Weddoes topped the British indie charts until they signed on to major RCA, and then they shot up the regular charts in England. In America, the band's success has been limited to college radio and small clubs, but for Weddoe fans, its music is like "Primal Scream" therapy.

There are, however, aspects of what the Wedding Present does that are linked directly to the spirit of the band's first full-length independent, import release, *George Best*. In 1992, in England, instead of just putting out an album, the band released a vinyl 45 each month for twelve months. Although the band's members were aware that they could sell large amounts of each 45, they restricted each single to a limited run; B-sides featured irreverent covers of a jumble of tracks ranging from the Monkees' "Pleasant Valley Sunday" to the Go-Betweens' "Cattle and Cane" to the *Twin Peaks* theme song, "Falling." The singles were then collected into two separately sold CDs called, sardonically (or not—since every one of those singles made it into the British top-30 singles chart) *Hit Parade 1* and *2*. In other words, they broke the rules: The establishment says that vinyl is dead, singles are dead, you're not supposed to release singles too often. And for their first two major-label albums, *Bizarro* and *Sea Monsters*, the band chose Steve Albini, whose trademark is a gory, apocalyptic guitar sound, as producer. Simply put, the band has made its business decisions without selling out, keeping original goals and focus intact.

By working within major-label systems, as the Wedding Present and the Fall have been, alternative bands have shown that not being on an independent label does not necessarily mean "selling out," particularly in the late eighties and early nineties. When Sonic Youth and later Nirvana signed to Geffen, fans feared sell-outs and sound changes. But by maintaining integrity to sound and image, both bands proved that working on their own terms through a major can, well, work. And a look at British indie bands, so many of whom go through American majors via licensing deals, shows that it's not fair to attach a stigma to a major anymore. Basically, if the kids, who are the ones who immediately pick up even the slightest hint of gimmick or superficiality, don't have a problem with alternative bands on majors, then chances are those majors are giving their bands plenty of space and control over their own work.

Which, when they're selling as many records as Nirvana does, they certainly deserve.

AMERICAN
FOUR
GUITAR
BANDS

Just as the British school of guitar bands captures a specific socio-logical mood and makeup through its sound and so appeals to fans who empathize with the actualization of that mood, the American school embodies a specific ethic and vibe. What the two schools have in common is not just the volume and energy of emergency in-your-face guitars but also the attitude that musicians should be real people (as opposed to big, distant stars) creating pure music with a base in a shared reality of performer and fan. Just as David Gedge or Mark E. Smith growl through their words with an unabashed, got-to-get-it-out-of-me, real man's vocal (or, perhaps more correctly, anti-vocal), so the lead singers of the three bands that are the focus of the current school of American alternative guitar bands — Dinosaur Jr., Sonic Youth (which actually has two members who switch off lead, one male, one female), and Nirvana — sing in their own voices to their own people: kids who feel stuck, hopeless, because life sucks and it won't change.

What makes the American and British schools distinct is that different social conditions have caused each to adopt a certain style of dress, be concerned with certain issues, live certain lifestyles—and thus, combined with the musical influences that are part of those conditions, develop a certain sound. On both continents, these musicians, starting from the point of star-as-everyman, live in situations that are similar to those of their fans, so there's empathy both ways. That bond gives this music an added poignancy for the kids who hear it. If the bands discussed in the previous chapter reek of cold, dank, former-British-Empire, late-twentieth-century England, then these American guitar bands are seeped with the U.S. version: discontentment and apathy in a land of malls and McDonald's, suburbs and stagnancy, *The Simpsons* and MTV. In 1977, the Clash sang "I'm So Bored with the U.S.A.," refusing to be taken in by the late-1970s view of America, à la television shows like *Charlie's Angels*, which also inundated British television and culture. In late eighties/early nineties America, the theme is simply "I'm so bored"—bored of being faced with a life trapped in a middle America riddled with unemployment and unhappiness. Just as bands like the Clash aimed to destroy modern television-propelled myths like rich over poor and glitz over mundanity, bands like Nirvana and Sonic Youth aim to expose the reality of American youth (untrusting, unfulfilled, dissatisfied) while ravaging pop music conformity (clean production, sweetly sung vocals) as violently as the late-seventies British punks did.

The three bands at the center of this American school—Dinosaur Jr., Sonic Youth, and Nirvana—aren't soundalike similar. They share some musical antecedents but not all, and they elicit different but congruent responses from fans; for that matter, their fans are similar but not entirely mutual. Nirvana, a much younger band than the other two, lacks the musical sophistication—however gritty it might be—of that pair but has had the larger-than-life impact that selling more than a million copies of *Nevermind* worldwide brings with it. Sonic Youth is more rooted in urban cool than most U.S. guitar bands. The band broadcasts influences ranging from Madonna (whose songs they covered under the name "Ciccone Youth" on their spoofingly titled *The Whitey Album*) to rappers Public Enemy, whose frontman Chuck D. cameoed on their major label debut *Goo*. Perhaps Dinosaur Jr., led by J Macsis (no period or J-A-Y, *please*—that would be as blandly "normal" as, say, stage clothes versus regular clothes or cleaned-up vocals), is the prototype American alternative guitar band, because it merges pop tunes with feedback, loud, loud guitars, barked-out vocals, and high school apathy à la *Fast Times at Ridgemont High* in equal doses. But these bands can certainly be seen as a group: In addition to sharing certain musical techniques and devices (like snarling, enraged guitars), they also share referents, many direct influences, and a similar fan makeup.

These bands' biggest common influence is the Stooges, featuring lead singer/squawker/stage-slither Iggy Pop. On albums like *Fun House* (which was originally released in 1970) and *Raw Power* (from 1973), the Stooges ripped through fast, hard, cathartically loud sheets of songs with the same energy as their musical descendants. Iggy's white-trash-boy-next-door-gone-bad looks and unkempt vocals have made him more than just musical mentor to bands like Dinosaur Jr. and Sonic Youth, which combine similar elements in their sound and stance. He's an alternative icon (just as, incidentally, the lead singers of those bands have become). Tracks like "Dirt," "Fun House," "I Wanna Be Your Dog," and "Search and Destroy" exemplify the band's roaring sound and, juxtaposed with albums like Sonic Youth's *Goo* or Dinosaur Jr.'s *Green Mind*, clearly show the impact the songs had on these younger bands.

However, the direct precursor of the American school of guitar bands were proto-hardcore groups like the Minutemen, Black Flag, and the Dead Kennedys in California: sloppy, loud bands formed by pissed-off guys with nowhere else to go. These seminal bands, formed in the late seventies and early eighties, sound sort of like raw fifties rock 'n' roll, but speeded up, exaggerated, furious, raised on TV and malls, and wacked out on one too many lines of cocaine. After the initial surge of late-seventies punk—both British and American—a different punk movement emerged. Its bands were formed most actively in southern California, although bands sprung up in other parts of the state as well, as San Francisco natives the Dead Kennedys show. Cali-punks weren't motivated by the same working-class, politicized anger of British punks or the bubble-gum-on-Dexedrine boppy fervor of the New York branch: They were driven by boredom, apathy, and an aversion to being stuck in a land of malls and Hollywood and artifice. If the Sex Pistols clanged on about "No Future," the California punks were more concerned about how they'd cope with the oppressively mundane status quo of the present.

The children of baby boomers and hippies, these bands grew up watching glitzed-out commercials and *The Brady Bunch*. Abba was the music of their teens. And so, just as Barbara Kruger and Jenny Holzer with their slogan-heavy, critical art draw on pop-cultured references, so California punk bands gave themselves names like the Dead Kennedys and Fear. After Johnny Rotten gnarled his way through political diatribes like "Anarchy in the U.K.," Black Flag screamed a song called "T.V. Party"—an almost frat-boy exultation of the joys of sitting around the television getting drunk with friends.

California punk was as much about aural anger as lyrical anger. Noise, machine-gun guitars, and an intentional, anti-traditional musical scream/vocal are common denominators of the Cali-punk sound (check out just about any Minutemen song, most of which are less than a minute long, to hear what I mean). California punks were as keen on shock value as British punks were: ripped clothes, pierced noses and nipples, tattoos, and big black combat boots were all de rigueur.

As loud and obnoxious as they were, the Cali-punks were speaking to a specific audience with its own dynamic: disinterested, no-where-to-go teenagers and twentysomethings, unchallenged, vaguely complacent, and bored shitless. Nirvana's core audience—as well as the band members themselves—are similarly disenfranchised. The Seattle sound yells with the same cleansing fury as California punk. It's a musical catharsis, plain and simple. What's labeled the Seattle sound—which includes the music of that city's natives like that of Soundgarden and Pearl Jam as well as that of Nirvana, from neighboring Aberdeen, Washington—is a product of working-class white kids pissed off at lives filled by unchallenging menial jobs or unemployment, unfulfilled with the shopping malls and suburbia that surround them. When Nirvana vocalist Kurt Cobain yells his lyrics, they're yells of despair, aggression, and the fury of "I want to escape."

Some critics have dubbed the kids who embody these emotions "slackers," after a film by the same name that traces the life of one typically goalless young man. Other, earlier films, like *Suburbia*, *River's Edge*, and *Repo Man*, all trace the bored inertia of these kids' lives, as does the book *Generation X* by Douglas Coupland. Once again, my term "kids" is one of attitude over age. Although most of the characters in those texts are not explicitly fans of the American guitar bands, they could well be: They dress like those fans (and the bands themselves—in ripped, faded plaid lumberjack shirts, t-shirts, and big dirty boots), live a similar, sluggish lifestyle of drinking beer and being bored without doing much of anything about it—lives that feel directionless. In fact, Superchunk sang about these kids, virtually exalting them, on its near-anthemic single "Slack Motherfucker."

In terms of where the slackers' heads are at, these kids—and there are huge numbers of them—equal passionate Grateful Dead or heavy-metal fans in musical devotion. The focus of their lives—the only thing that matters—becomes their favorite bands' music—along with all that goes with it, like dressing like the members of their favorite bands and going to their gigs. The metal analogy is particularly close: Metal lyrics often deal with the same issues of dissatisfaction as punk/alternative ones do. Metal also uses volume and snarled guitars and anger to get its point across. Metal kids, like alternative fans, have a distinctive look, style, way of dancing. The typical metal fashion components are long hair, black leather jackets, and spikes; slackers, in contrast, are into faded flannel shirts, often with their sleeves ripped off, and Doc Martens—bulky orthopedic-shoes-gone-bad. There is a sense of doom and violence in the metal look and stance; slackers look more like just-woke-up college students. While metal kids often look grim or suicidal, slackers look too bored to do much more than just hang out.

Although the main feature of the slacker look is its cheap, no-frills utilitarianism, haute couture absurdly latched on to it post-Nirvana. Once grunge hit, there were Chanel versions of Doc Martens, complete with trademark double C's; a feature on grunge fashion in American *Vogue*, accompanied by text written by SubPop copresident Jonathan Poneman; and pricey silk versions of army-and-navy flannel shirts designed by Perry Ellis designer Marc Jacobs. All of a sudden, Doc Martens were for sale in Bloomingdales and the grunge look was splashed in mainstream shop windows. Initially, grunge fashions—affordable, sturdy, rugged—were the perfect accompaniment to the bare-bones, populist music of bands like Nirvana. To mutate that ethic into something fleetingly trendy, expensive-fragile, is to actively disrespect it, to turn it inside out. It's like doing an expensive disco remix of a Nirvana demo. It's taking something pure, gritty—and cheap—and making it slick and produced. If the open wound of Kurt Cobain's voice is an assault on the Whitney Houstons of the world, couture-ing his look is an inadvertent assault on that growl. And yet, in the throes of a global reces-

AMERICAN
GUITAR
BANDS
63

sion, perhaps the only way couture can have any relevance is to strip it of its glitz. In other words, if a Chanel suit was appropriate high fashion in the high-living eighties, combatesque, clunky boots seem just right for the more austere nineties.

Both grunge and metal fans wear t-shirts emblazoned with their favorite bands' names. But t-shirts for bands like Dinosaur Jr., Nirvana, and Sonic Youth usually have a clear visual or linguistic message. For example, Dinosaur Jr.'s 1991 tour in support of *Green Mind* featured t-shirts with a bright picture of a cow's head. Nirvana's t-shirts for the *Nevermind* tour had a black background and the band's name in bright, crisp, formal letters on the front; on the back, there was a disturbing, drunk-looking smiley face and the slogan—lest any of their fans think they sold out by moving from indie label SubPop to mega-major DGC—"Flower Sniffin Kitty Pettin' Baby Kissin' Corporate Rock Whores." A frequently seen Sonic Youth t-shirt features the ominous invocation "Kill Your Idols." These images may seem brutal, obtuse, or word-heavy messages, but they contrast strongly—and so distinguish the kids who wear them—from heavy metal t-shirt wearers, whose attire features muddier imagery, as can be seen from the album cover–based graphics of t-shirts promoting metal bands like AC/DC and Motley Crue. To me (who admittedly is coming from an alternative instead of metal angle), it's the difference between Barbara Kruger's think-about-it slogans and one-dimensional graffiti.

Although the differences between each genre's t-shirts may seem slight or even forced, they are anything but that to fans of either genre. To a die-hard fan of metal or American guitar bands or the Grateful Dead or whomever, to wear the wrong t-shirt is unthinkable (which is why, inversely, there's so much money to be made in music t-shirt sales—to wear the right t-shirt is all-important). And just as fans know almost instinctively what to them is cool and what isn't musically, they are drawn to whatever fashion statement feels right. And, just as listening to the same bands or smoking illicit cigarettes after school makes you one of the gang, liking the "right" bands (which are another crowd's wrong bands) makes you fit in. Wearing a t-shirt proclaiming your allegiance to one of these bands identifies who you hang out with (and what that represents, as in the cool kids, the nerds, the dropouts, the drug users, etc.) in the same way a skinhead haircut or (on the contrary) a team letter jacket would. To conform to a group of kids—and so to fit in, which is what every adolescent longs to do, as long as fitting in doesn't include parents—is as much about look as ideology or action. To pierce your nipple or your nose and listen to Dinosaur Jr. instead of Guns 'n' Roses is as conformist as the actions of a more mainstream, conformist kid. It's just conforming to a different group and code of behavior. Which is why the distinctions of sound, fashion, and attitude between the groups is so important. Identity within a group, which can be represented by something as subtle as a certain t-shirt, defines kids who feel that mainstream society doesn't speak to them.

The metal connection is a key one. For kids who feel like outsiders, the volume and nihilism of heavy metal and its imagery is often an appealing escape. Witness the well-known case examined in the documentary film *Dream Deceivers*, where two Utah teenaged Judas Priest fans shot themselves in a suicide pact that their parents later attributed to the music. Although alternative kids feel as locked into their situations as metal kids do, their music lacks metal's nihilism. In spite of the prevalence of loud guitars and often grim lyrics in the music of these alternative bands, the American school of guitar bands is as much about hope and making a change, or at least finding a refuge from the entrapment of the world, as it is about aggression. And, while metal bands frequently coat their music with morbid imagery, alternative bands concentrate on releasing adolescent tension and aggressions rather than on death. As much as it's about venting that energy, alternative music is also about band members' being real people who are close to their audience instead of being stars of high-tech light shows in big mega-stadiums. Such values are antithetical to the overall presentations of metal artists like Ozzy Osborne, Judas Priest, and Motley Crue.

But the American alternative guitar bands—hey, let's be real, alternative bands in general—look different, are younger, are more ever-evolving than metal. They also play a less self-centered music. The Minutemen use elements of jazz and blues. Half of Sonic Youth played in Glenn Branca's avant-jazz band. And, really, the core of Nirvana's best songs, of Dinosaur Jr. songs like "The Wagon" and "Freak Scene," and of Sonic Youth tracks like "Teen Age Riot," is good old-fashioned pop songs, stuck in your head like chewing gum on your shoe even though, in the case of these bands, they're covered with a finish of guitars or feedback or mangled vocals or all of the above. But what all these bands can offer kids who feel that they don't fit into mainstream society—just as metal bands can—is the coherence of an all-inclusive fan makeup. For these fans, the music creates the one oasis where they can feel they belong.

Within that specific subculture, behaviors that might seem strange or inappropriate outside the context of that scene become acceptable. A key example is slam-dancing, which California punks did regularly. Slamming has evolved into a seemingly aggressive style of dancing called moshing (an offshoot that I'll discuss later in detail, as it has become a given at American guitar bands' gigs). Slamming still goes on but is primarily done at very hardcore punk shows. Slam dancing is what it sounds like: kids running into each other, hitting their bodies full force against each other. It takes place down near the front of the stage in an improvised area known as the pit. As violent as this activity may sound, it is purely an energy release. For music that confronts, dares, and attacks its audience with volume and speed, there is no dance more appropriate than slamming. And at punk shows it's nearly impossible, in contrast with mellower or more traditional rock shows, to stay seated, let alone sit still.

Slamming was as common at California punk shows as it was at the gigs of another seminal American guitar band: Hüsker Dü. Although the Minneapolis-based band was not, strictly speaking, part of the Cali-punk movement, Hüsker Dü laid the groundwork for many other bands, including Dinosaur Jr., Nirvana, and, to a lesser extent, Sonic Youth (the Sonics' first releases came out simultaneous with the Hüskers'). The Hüskers' distinctive sound, which has since been frequently imitated, revolves around classic melodies that have been tensed up enough to make even the calmest listener sweat. It's as if the band has taken a Beatles outtake, sped it up, screamed out its vocals, and infused it with anger and force. There is also, even deeper, a connection to the Byrds, Neil Young, sometime Byrd/sometime Flying Burrito Brother Gram Parsons: The sound is a blend of sweet folk twang, a heap of country, and precipitant guitars. Loud, loud guitars rip through songs, drums propel the music fast enough to be edgy but slow enough to linger, and lead singer Bob Mould's voice (or is that anti-voice?) grinds away in angst. Early Hüsker Dü records, like 1983's *Metal Circus* and 1984's *Zen Arcade* (both on indie SST), sound as vital today as they did when they first came out. And maybe even more so: Indeed, the same formula of pop song with rage icing is what gave Nirvana its huge success. It's no wonder that Mould's post–Hüsker Dü band, Sugar, has become such a major alternative success; when it released its debut LP,

Copper Blue, in circa–grunge 1992, the music demonstrated the new techniques like a math teacher showing his students how to solve puzzling equations.

Check out classic tracks like "Makes No Sense" or "Hate Paper Doll" (both off 1985's *Flip Your Wig*) and you'll get the Hüskers' blend of pop and heavy grunge, a decidedly alternative mix. If that's not clear enough, their choice of covers should be: the Byrds' "Eight Miles High" and the Beatles' "Ticket To Ride." To express their roots and speak to their fans, the band gives each song heavy treatment to reinterpret each as a means to escape the unescapable world of teenage boredom and inertia.

As three normal midwestern guys, the band offers its audience an easy-to-empathize-with, no-bullshit presentation. Three big beefy guys — anti-frontman frontman, plain-old-guy Bob Mould; teddy-bear drummer Grant Hart, who later started his own band, Nova Mob; and then bass player Greg Norton, whose distinguishing feature was a huge handlebar mustache — simply got on the stage, wearing their no-frills clothes, and played with as much energy and emotion as a classic soul singer. It's important to draw the distinction between *lack of image* (or even total lack of fashion statement), as is the case with the Hüskers, and *anti-fashion*, which is what British, New York, and California punks were into. It's impossible to ignore the theatricality of, say, the Clash's splattered trousers or the Ramones' identical black leather biker jackets (the 1977 punk rock equivalent of the Beatles' identical suits, circa 1964) or the L.A. punks' safety pins and rips. These all are examples of blatant, "look at me" clothes, albeit "look at me, I'm different" clothes. Hüsker Dü, and the bands that have followed in its footsteps, as well as their fans, said, "Don't look — listen to the music instead." So, in addition to shunning musical conventions and the mainstream, the band also shunned the concept of a focus on visual presentation. Oblivious to image or even, in a sense, to audience, they were merely themselves; that anti-image approach was picked up by all three of the main bands discussed in this chapter: Dinosaur Jr., Sonic Youth, and Nirvana.

Let's begin with the band that most strongly follows in the Hüsker Dü tradition: Dinosaur Jr. Dinosaur (the band added the "Jr." to its name after releasing its self-titled debut and being threatened with a lawsuit by a sixties band with the same name) churns with the same insurgent guitars that constantly propel the music forward. There is one salient difference, however: the lead vocals of J Mascis. If the Fall's Mark E. Smith is the anti-hero of the British school of guitar bands, then his U.S. counterpart is Mascis: long hair dripping down his face, sort of singing, struggling in a spazzed-out warble to reach major chunks of register in each song. And while some other singer might try to cover up his weaknesses, Mascis seems to revel in them: On tracks like *Green Mind*'s "I Live for That Look" and *You're Living All Over Me*'s "In a Jar," he swerves around notes like a drunk driver making too-wide turns. Mascis is like a rebellious kid pushing the limits with parents; it's as if he is taunting some mainstream listener to object to his singing style, to tell him to sing properly. He constantly reiterates and basks in his alternative identity and its opposition to the mainstream. Like those of Mark E. Smith or the Wedding Present's David Gedge, the farther away Mascis's vocals move from conventional singing, the more drive and angsted-out energy the songs seem to have. It's as if hitting notes in a traditionally beautiful way would add extra baggage that would slow the song down.

Some of Dinosaur Jr.'s songs, like "Freak Scene," "The Wagon," and "Puke + Cry," use pop music conventions like hooks and anthemic choruses just as an accessible, standard top-40 song would. But by energizing those elements, by bending them and personalizing them to speak to Dinosaur's "we're alternative" fans (in the same way that Mascis bends the notes he's hitting with his scraggly voice), the band incites its audience by musical means to question its past and current reality, to take from it what they will, to make it their own. The fact that Dinosaur Jr.'s members present themselves as real people further encourages this participation.

By singing in his admittedly flawed, anti-star voice, by appearing (as Hüsker Dü did) in real-life clothes, with unkempt hair, devoid of even the slightest hint of manufacture or pretense, Mascis does the same thing as Shelagh Delaney did in "A Taste of Honey," Harold Pinter in "The Homecoming," and Alice Walker in *The Color Purple*. By concentrating on the lives of working-class people, each writer proves these lives are as complex and meaty and fascinating as those of the rich and famous, that the grit of the everyday is as engrossing as fantasy, and that what the Clash called "gutter smarts" in "Garageland"—that which you learn outside of school, on the streets—can be as valid as a more refined education.

Perhaps the clearest statement of Dinosaur Jr. as a band made

Dinosaur Jr.'s anti-icon J Mascis

up of real, frill-free people is their choice of cover versions and the way they do them. On *You're Living All Over Me,* they cover Peter Frampton's "Show Me the Way"—a mainstream, bland, FM hit. Twisted on its side Mascis style, it is un-sung, off-key, almost tongue-in-cheek, overpiled with extra-loud guitars like an over-stuffed deli sandwich. It's as if Mascis is saying, "We know it's bad, but fuck definitions of bad and good—let's party." On the B-side of the British "Get Me" single, he rips apart the Flying Burrito Broth-ers' "Hot Burrito #2," staggering through its vocals like a drunk stumbling home from a night on the town. The band's treatment of these covers is the musical equivalent of Cindy Sherman's early movie stills, in which the artist enters the world of what he or she is covering (in Sherman's case, the heavily posed world of forties and fifties B-movie stills) and nearly negates it by his or her mere pres-ence.

Another cover the band does pokes at the alternative establish-ment itself. If bands with the spike and punch of Dinosaur Jr. and Sonic Youth embody the true definition of alternative, then bands like Depeche Mode, R.E.M., and the Cure—with their slightly safer, sweeter sound—edge closer to the mainstream, what I'd dub oxy-moronically "the alternative establishment." It's not that this latter category of bands isn't alternative per se – they do twist mainstream expectations. It's just that they do it in a less confrontational way – and consequently, they appeal to a broader audience than do spikier bands. They add quirky instead of aggressive details to standard pop constructions. On Dinosaur Jr.'s cover of the Cure's "Just Like Heaven," deep, insidious bass lines poison the song's hook, the fedback twang of gnarled guitars is emphasized heavily in the mix, and then there's Mascis's voice – at one point doubled for a split second in a virtual belch and hiss up into a scream. The Dinosaur Jr. version is like an aural kick in the Cure's balls: It emphasizes the grit of American guitar bands versus the gleam of techno-pop alternative bands like the Cure. It's as much a tribute as a violent attack; it's basically a Dinosaur Jr. fan taking a Cure t-shirt, holding it in the air, and then ripping it cruelly in half.

Once again, Mascis is almost anti-singing, and once again, the song is necessarily permeated with the sounds of its surroundings. If Mark E. Smith's voice is like a dark cup of tea on a rainy day in Manchester, Mascis's suggests a cold bottle of Rolling Rock at a truck stop in Massachusetts, where Dinosaur Jr. is based. Dinosaur Jr. – pop tunes screeched through a shaky voice and endless guitars – is the voice of wanting to escape but not being able to. In lieu of an actual escape, the only exit from mundane surroundings is via clanging guitars. Looking and sounding the stoner, the potential pot-smoking dropout in the back of a classroom, J pairs his grainy warble with the sort of impending guitars which offer some catharsis from that status quo.

There's an almost joyous buoyance on trademark Dinosaur Jr. tracks like "The Wagon," off the band's label debut, *Green Mind*, and the old-fashioned jukebox-memorable "Freak Scene," from 1988's *Bug* LP. Nonetheless, something dark and heavy is going on as well – it's the sound of knowing there's something ominous counteracting the blissful oasis. Although they ring with a somewhat clearer sound than the earlier songs, tracks off 1993's *Where You Been*, like "Get Me" and "Start Choppin'," similarly balance exuberance and grit. Consistently, Dinosaur Jr.'s tracks are almost excessively guitared-out, often featuring or ending in long solos. The band uses growling guitars to pound through pain just as a band like the Wedding Present does. Except that, whereas a band like the Wedding Present frazzles itself into a whizzing guitar frenzy, J's solos are somehow fast and languid; they saunter, Neil Young style, beautifully bopping through notes as if they want to linger in their catharsis as long as possible.

One of Dinosaur Jr.'s original members, Lou Barlow, left in 1989, before the *Green Mind* LP was recorded, to concentrate on his own (wonderful, perverse, odd, but charming) band, Sebadoh, which takes some of his first band's alternative techniques—ratty, real vocals, loud, grinding guitars—and builds on them. Sebadoh not only works within alternative systems, it luxuriates in them: bouncing from indie label to indie label with releases on everything from SubPop to Homestead to small indie Dark Beloved Cloud; cluttering some albums with snippets and half-songs (on *The Freed Man*, in particular); recording low-fi and shabby to give some studio sessions the sound quality of a homemade bootleg; releasing acoustic sessions on indie labels like Shrimper under the name Sentridoh. And so the band twists conventions several rungs farther from the mainstream than even Dinosaur Jr. does on its post-Barlow, major-label albums. Yet, just like Dinosaur Jr., underneath the no-frills layers there is often—as on *Smash Your Head on the Punk Rock*'s "Brand New Love" and *Bubble and Scrape*'s "Soul and Fire"—a bona fide pop song. And on a cultural level, Sebadoh and Dinosaur Jr. do the same thing: take the preconceptions of mainstream rock and humanize them, intensify them, re-address them to speak to their thrift-store-clothed, beer-drinking contemporaries.

Dinosaur Jr. has directly influenced a handful of bands, although most of them mollify the surge of Dinosaur's fury somewhat. Buffalo Tom is one of these. This band, from Boston, not only brought in J Mascis as coproducer of its first album, *Birdbrain*, but also used the same studio (Fort Apache, in Boston) and engineers (Sean Slade and Paul Kolderie) as Dinosaur did. The sound is similar but not identical. Tom lead singer Bill Janovitz is not as flashy vocally (or is that anti-vocally?) as Mascis is. While the vocals are not exactly mixed down, they are not featured as more important than the ringing guitars with which they're combined. And those guitars are less furied and more conventionally beautiful than Dinosaur Jr.'s. They repeatedly ring with rootsy influences like the Flying Burrito Brothers and Neil Young. Certainly, the sound is never crystal-clear refined. Even on 1992's comparatively crisp *Let Me Come Over* LP, it is still as ragged as the frayed ends of a flannel shirt. But Buffalo Tom's sound is more expansive, less uptight jolted-raucous than Dinosaur Jr.'s. And frequently, Tom's lyrics are more about love and relationships than Mascis's are. For examples, compare simple song titles like "Caress" and "Bleeding Heart" with Dinosaur tracks like "Thumb," "Muck," "Lose," and "The Lung." By dealing with conventional pop song fare, the band is one rung less scary/different/alternative than Dinosaur Jr. is.

Which is not to imply that the band is not alternative—it is. Dressed in the thrift-store clothes its fans wear, playing no-frills music without superclean vocals or toned-down guitars, the band has a real-life charm that seems almost antithetical to what's on the top-40 charts, particularly pre-Nirvana. Those qualities are clearly illustrated in its key cover version of the Psychedelic Furs' "Heaven," which is an extra bonus track on the *Birdbrain* CD. Once again, the band covers a song by a group from the more mainstream end of the alternative realm, and once again subverts it to make the song its own, via nontraditional everyman vocals and too-assertive guitars. Just as Dinosaur Jr. ditched the Cure's "synthesized" ornateness in its version of that band's "Just Like Heaven," Buffalo Tom's take on the Furs' song favors sincerity, simplicity, and reality over big-budget production.

In the same realm, also known for some "cut the bullshit" covers, are the Lemonheads. The band, also from Boston, has worked with Paul Kolderie as well. Led by Evan Dando, the band is less about the cathartic power of loud guitars than Dinosaur Jr. is, although thrashing, sloppy-cool guitars are a large part of what they do. The Heads are more rooted in stick-in-your-head songwriting than many of their contemporaries are—even if their songs are frequently more like songwriting scribbles than full songs (as on the bulk of *It's a Shame About Ray*). Veering closer to pop tradition and slightly farther from the roar of feedback and guitars, the band has evolved from making early snotty-kid albums like *Hate Your Friends* and *Creator* (which came out on Boston indie Taang in 1987 and 1988, respectively) into a power-pop band for the nineties. Dando, with his vacant stoner stare and lazy good looks, has been molded by the press into a grunge teen idol. The band's more recent material fuses bite with sing-along tunes as well, as is exemplifed by *Lick*'s "Mallo Cup," *Lovey*'s "Stove," and *It's a Shame About Ray*'s "My Drug Buddy" and "Rudderless."

The way the band takes existing songs and warps them really embodies the alternative ethic. Take, for example, the Lemonheads' version of Suzanne Vega's murky "Luka" (off *Lick*), which forcefully contorts the swingy, almost masked tale of child abuse into a brutal, chugging cry for help; on CD copies of *Lick*, the band growls through an equally forceful version of, of all things, Patsy Cline's "Strange." The band also covers—with a taunting smile—everything from "Frank Mills" from the musical *Hair* (on *It's a Shame About Ray*) to Kiss' "Plaster Caster" to Simon and Garfunkel's "Mrs. Robinson"; the juxtaposition of all these covers—and the smash-it-up way they're interpreted by the band—is like flipping the cable TV channels all night: energized, cacophonous, occasionally abrasive, and very late twentieth century. These covers shun conventions like pristine vocals and controlled guitars to make these songs theirs, grunging them up as if to say, "Even a punked-out band like us can cover something as beautiful as a song by Patsy Cline," in a way that is intrinsically postmodern. Even their more respectful, less assertive covers, like their version of Linda Ronstadt's "Different Drum" off the *Famous Spanish Dishes* EP, their more recent version of Simon and Garfunkel's "Mrs. Robinson," or their *Lovey* take on Gram Parsons's "Brass Buttons," break that preconceived distinction between establishment rock 'n' roll and the alternative realm. And, of course, the bands that bridge that gap most effectively—R.E.M., the Cure, Depeche Mode—are the ones that span several fan bases and so appeal to more than the alternative core, sell more records, play bigger venues, get written about in bigger magazines, etc.

Uncle Tupelo may not be from the Boston area, but its sound evokes a similar sense of Americana. Although its first two albums were produced at Fort Apache by Kolderie and Slade, and the band is musically in the Gram-Parsons-meets-Hüsker-Dü territory, Tupelo's members are from Belleville, Illinois, a depressed suburb of St. Louis, Missouri. Although the band is musically far removed from Nirvana, its lyrics, which speak of the members' own surroundings, cover similar territory: being unemployed, working on a factory line, getting drunk as the only escape. The song titles alone— "Whiskey Bottle," "Gun," "Looking for a Way Out," "Factory Belt," "Punch Drunk"—convey the scene. In their own way, these songs create images as potent and depressed as those in John Steinbeck's *The Grapes of Wrath*—images of a hand-to-mouth existence. Tupelo members express the dynamics of their surroundings with the clarity and desperation of rap artists like Ice-T, Public Enemy, and Ice Cube singing of the problems in the urban neighborhoods in which they live. Like rap, Tupelo's music speaks with vividness and poignancy.

It's impossible to mention bands like Dinosaur Jr. and its musical progeny without mentioning Neil Young. His rootsy, twanging-but-enraged guitars are a key, necessary influence on these bands' musicianship. From the juxtaposition of gritty vocals and resplendent guitars on an early album like *Everybody Knows This Is Nowhere* to the almost soul-like darkness of chunks of *Tonight's the Night* and *Harvest*, Young's pure, everyman style is at the core of what these bands do. He has an almost tangible American-ness—as do other influences on these bands, like Gram Parsons, the Flying Burrito Brothers, and Creedence Clearwater Revival, whose *Green River* LP was the namesake of a Seattle-based proto-grunge band that paved the way for Nirvana, as well as other Seattle bands like Mudhoney, Soundgarden, and the Screaming Trees. It's the expression of truck-stop-and-K-mart, real-life America, seeping through notes of Young's guitar. This slice of reality is part of the appeal of J Mascis, Uncle Tupelo, Buffalo Tom, and, hey, everyone from Bruce Springsteen to Garth Brooks. They're the guys next door, on line at the 7-Eleven, shooting pool in the back room of the local bar, singing about everyday problems in a voice you can understand.

While a band like Dinosaur Jr. or Hüsker Dü expresses a down-home American dynamic, Sonic Youth is distinctly urban—more correctly, distinctly New York. The band and its four idiosyncratic members—Thurston Moore on guitar and vocals, Kim Gordon on bass guitar and vocals, Lee Renaldo on guitar, and drummer Steve Shelley, who replaced several previous drummers—simply ooze downtown New York City attitude, street smarts, artiness, brutality, and grit. Although their most recent work, like "100%" and "Youth Against Fascism" from their second DGC album, *Dirty*, uses some standard pop structures like verse-chorus-verse, the bulk of the Youth's work has been not just about bending pop conventions but violently breaking them, spitting on them, and throwing them out the window.

Part of that aggressive denial of preconceptions comes from the band's roots; both Moore and Renaldo played with Glenn Branca, an avant-garde musician who instructed the guitarists in his band to play with unconventional guitar tunings so that their playing sounded, to ears used to more standard tunings, off-key, off-kilter, just plain wrong. Those tunings, which are antithetical to virtually all the ones in Western pop music that preceded them, are the foundation of Sonic Youth's sound and also the key to the band's philosophy. Like the juxtaposition of a thrift-store t-shirt with designer

Half of Sonic Youth: Lee Renaldo and "cosmo girl from hell" Kim Gordon

trousers, the Youth blend classic rock 'n' roll with guitar tunings that could previously be heard only on some Eastern instruments and in avant-garde Western forms. Frequently, the band mixes musical conconctions that might seem illogical on paper: Dissonant guitars demolish Iggy Pop and the Stooges "I Wanna Be Your Dog," Public Enemy leader Chuck D. raps with the band, and there are heavy political lyrics on one of the band's poppiest-ever tracks, "Youth Against Fascism." Playing with a vast array of musical elements, Sonic Youth tries them out and so customizes them like a hand tailored suit, albeit a suit with scraggly strings and rough edges intentionally left in. Where the members of another band might be worried if their music included long sections of discordant notes, deep feedback, and just plain noise, Sonic Youth piles them on. Where there are rules, they are meant to be broken; where there are not, there's open territory ready to be explored.

Sonic Youth members have also—particularly in their early work—rejected standard verse-verse-chorus-verse pop music structures. In fact, early albums like *Bad Moon Rising*, which came out on Homestead in 1985, and *Evol* ("love" backwards, for the uninitiated), which SST Records released in 1986, use an almost jazz-based improvisation and end-of-song, anti-structured jamming. The songs have an amorphic structure: It feels as though each song's composition depends more on the band's mood when it's played than on notes written on a page. Improvisation is still part of the band's live shows and of its more recent work—for example, listen to the frazzled guitar improvisation on tracks from 1992's *Dirty* such as "Theresa's Sound-world" and "On the Strip." Even on tracks with a stricter form, like "Teen Age Riot" or "Schizophrenia" (off the 1987 *Sister* LP), there are twists that make the songs not only alternative—because they lead toward an expectation and then veer speedily off that path—but Sonic Youthed, because they incorporate the band's indelible trademarks: the oddly tuned guitar, near-spoken, warts-and-all vocals, and the sheer drive of someone on a race to escape.

On many tracks, like "Swimsuit Issue" (from *Dirty*) and "(I Got A) Catholic Block," the guitars sound like a charging machine gun—blasting away convention, blasting away sweetness and light/pretty/disposable pop songs, blasting their fans into action. That loud boom of beating drums and guitars, whether live or on record, feels almost literally violent: loud and focused and pounding like a drill again and again and again. (Play the first thirty seconds of *Dirty* tracks like "Swimsuit Issue" or the near-end of "Theresa's Sound-world" if you want proof.) For fans brought up on TV news death footage, police brutality, and gang wars, there is an alarming appropriateness to that musical thrust. In other words, if Gene Pitney was the right soundtrack for the "Ozzie and Harriet" generation, then Sonic Youth is the right soundtrack for kids raised on *Rambo*. The band's aggressive side is even more vivid live than on record. Particularly from Moore, who mangles his instrument, ripping at it violently from above and below as if it were a bug bite. Pulling his guitar onto the stage floor, he seems to be pulled himself by its sheer force, like a small woman walking a huge dog. If part of the goal of the band's music, for both themselves and their fans, is to release bottled-up anger, they've achieved it.

As Dinosaur Jr. features the anti-vocals of J Mascis, Sonic Youth's lead vocals are traded off between two nontraditional singers: Thurston Moore and Kim Gordon. Moore's singing is reminiscent of Mascis's in that he warbles to reach certain notes. But his voice is drier, less keen to hog the spotlight. He sings to get out his lyrics and have something to accompany the fury of his guitar, without beauty or excess. "Singing" isn't even really the way to describe it—Moore spits out his words like a teenage boy mouthing into his bathroom mirror, needing to get the words out, intent on all the rebellious things he's saying. And that bad-boy adolescent image is reinforced by Moore on a stage: little-kid face, Dennis the Menace hair, t-shirt, and Converse all-stars, seemingly demolishing his guitar to get out the notes.

Gordon's voice is even drier but craves the spotlight; it's a deadpan combination of attitude, confidence, and an "I dare you" mix of balls and femininity. This is best illustrated on tracks like the *Goo* LP's "Kool Thing" and *Dirty*'s "JC." It's not about conventional beauty but more about power: as, incidentally, is Gordon's public persona. Sexy clothes like short shorts and tight t-shirts are more about the freedom to wear whatever one wants and still be a tough player – regardless of sex – than sex appeal. But while the guitarists in a band like My Bloody Valentine are de-sexed, Gordon's sexuality is present – it's just something that she controls consciously, just as Madonna controls her public persona. And her sassy delivery of some of her lyrics – "Don't ever call me mom" on "JC"; "Don't touch my breast" and "I ain't giving you head" screamed on "Swimsuit Issue" – reiterates that strength. Like a *Cosmo* girl from Hell, Gordon entices her audience with her suggestive clothing and almost taunting speak/singing. As enticing as it may get, however, you never forget that she calls the shots.

Often, her tone is give-me-a-break cynical. It's reminiscent of some of the language that word-heavy artists like Jenny Holzer and Barbara Kruger use. (In the former's work: "Protect me from what I want"; in the latter's: "We don't need another hero," "I shop therefore I am.") Sometimes, Gordon's lines and delivery seem like they could be outtakes from Holzer's or Kruger's workbook. On *Daydream Nation*'s "The Sprawl," she asks (almost dares) her listeners "Does this sound simple? Fuck you. Is this for sale?" On *Dirty*'s "Drunken Butterfly," she repeats, like a sex addict's bible verse, "I love you – what's your name?" Many of the songs Gordon sings deal with problems that modern women face, without ever holding back. On *Goo*'s "Tunic (Song for Karen)" she examines Karen Carpenter's fatal anorexia. Another song off that album, "Swimsuit Issue," explores sexual harassment. Gordon's frankness in dealing with these issues is mirrored by films like *Thelma and Louise* and *Gas, Food, Lodging*. Treated with neither fanfare nor restraint, women's issues are approached because they affect the lives of the writers of these texts and their audience.

A lot is made in the alternative world of the impact Gordon has had as a role model for other bands. In the wake of Sonic Youth circa *Daydream Nation* (1988) through the early nineties, a slew of all-female, heavy alternative bands, sometimes called "foxcore" bands by the press, have popped up. These groups often go by names that deal with their Gordon-esque brand of feminist-femininity ironically or through double entendre: Examples include Babes in Toyland, Hole, L7, Lunachicks. These bands are important on a cultural level because they reject the stereotype of women as demure and innocent. Often dressed in little girls' dresses paired with "don't-fuck-with-me" Doc Martens unisex boots, these guitar bands bolt with an intensity that never makes concessions to being female. They feature gory, loud guitars and emergencied vocals. Sometimes, as with Hole, those vocals are close to Gordon's nearspeak. Sometimes, as with a band like L7, they are more traditionally sung. One thing's for sure: These ain't no Go-Go's. And just as their look implies that a woman's reality is not all the sweet submissive sexuality of the top-40 pop queens, their lyrics are filled with gritty, sometimes painfully frank but usually matter-of-fact details of the intimacies of women's lives. The Lunachicks have a song called "Plugg" about menstruation, and their second album is called *Binge and Purge*, referring to eating disorders. L7's self-explanatory song titles include "Diet Pill" and "This Ain't Pleasure." Comparing their almost brutal approach to real life with the cooing, soft vocals of Whitney Houston or Paula Abdul, who sing boy-meets-girl stories, is like trying to square twelve-year-olds having to deal with condoms to prevent contracting the AIDS virus with kids who are still playing with Barbie and Ken dolls.

I include these female American guitar bands here, in the midst of my discussion of Sonic Youth, because, although many critics have lumped them in with the American grunge scene of heavy, all-male bands like Nirvana, Mudhoney, the Afghan Whigs, et al., I see them as having a stronger link to the hip, harsh, but sexy femininity/feminism of Kim Gordon. Certainly, the overall sound and age of bands like L7 and Babes in Toyland is closer to Nirvana's, but if you're going to categorize these bands by their sex and their direct and semiotic approach to that sex, they belong with Gordon. These younger women approach their sexuality in a way that parallels Gordon's stance; it's as if they're saying, "We're women and we can be sexy—but so what? we're also tougher than tough." For Gordon and the women who've followed in her path, that attitude is reflected in music, lyrics, and fashion sense.

They also belong alongside artists from Cindy Sherman—who

comments on outdated ways of viewing women in her series of simu-
lated B-movie stills — to Karen Finley — who criticizes the objectifying
of women in her performance pieces. But many women in alternative
music comment through more than just their music. Babes in
Toyland lead singer Kat Bjelland and Hole lead singer Courtney
Love regularly wear near-Victorian, three-sizes-too-small baby doll
dresses, big boots, and too too much red lipstick: The look is somewhere between punk rock Betty Boop and a rag doll on LSD. Love
often even writes provocative slogans on her skin in lipstick — like
"mother" when she was pregnant with her first child. Simply put, the
mark acts as post-feminist tattoo. As powerful, commanding women
appropriating clothing that typically represents demure, soft-and-
sweet feminity but twisting it so they control it instead of it defining
them, these singers are not only declaring their strength but — hey —
doing exactly what their music does: taking a traditional form and
bending/contorting/jolting it into a form that is relevant to them and
their lives.

And although Kim Gordon is a contemporary influence for the
so-called foxcore bands, there are certainly others. In the late seven-
tiess in New York City, Patti Smith and Blondie's Debbie Harry
played with preconceived notions of femininity and sexiness and
came out with their own proportions of both. In circa punk England,
the Slits examined the same issues with an irony and attitude that
would seem at home on a Lunachicks or L7 lyric sheet or album
cover; in early-eighties England, the Au Pairs and the Delta 5 featured too-tough women singers denying the validity of female stereotypes. All turned the image of the clean, glossy, neatly groomed and
made-up woman pop star inside out. Sort of the Bangles-gone-
grunge, bands like L7 and Babes in Toyland tip their hats to female
stereotypes and then aggressively (as is the postmodern way) refuse
to buy into them.

A more recent school of bands, the Riot Grrrls, are clearly in
debt to role models like Kim Gordon. A small movement of growling,
almost whining young female-fronted bands, the Riot Grrrls are
closer musically — not to mention in terms of images and fashion
sense — to bands like the Delta 5 and the late-seventies British punk
band X-Ray Spex, which featured the animalesque squawk and
consumer-cynical lyrics of lead singer Poly Styrene. Riot Grrrl
bands have cynical, taunting names like Bikini Kill, Bratmobile, and
Heavens to Betsy; they bask in a "don't-fuck-with-me" attitude

along the lines of Gordon's. With members' ages hovering around the twenty mark, they're equal parts *Ms.* and *Sassy*. Expressing their preachy, often lesbian-focused, nineties-radical-feminist dialectic via fanzines, singles on indie labels, virtually exclusively college radio airplay, and small-club gigs, Riot Grrrls (who have some British sister bands, like Huggy Bear and Mambo Taxi) exemplify alternative musical systems at work. Yet, although their stance (and, more often than not, their deadpan, anti-beautiful vocals) parallels Kim Gordon's, their music for the most part doesn't have the depth of Sonic Youth's. Rooted, particularly vocally, in seventies punk bands like X-Ray Spex and Penetration, Riot Grrrls are more about youthful, angry energy than songwriting or record-it-for-posterity longevity.

Sonic Youth similarly deals with the issues in its members' own lives: a friend being shot ("100%"), feeling that life is going nowhere, with no escape ("Society Is a Hole"), boredom ("Teen Age Riot"). The band uses the language of its peers and its culture — words like "sucks" and "fuck" crop up again and again. Certainly, that language breaks "it's-got-to-be-clean-enough-to-get-radio-airplay" pop music convention, but its importance goes further. If you accept what Sonic Youth does as art — as I do, unquestionably — then using real-world language and situations defines those everyday situations as valid source material for art. It implies, as John Berger more explicitly outlines in his book, *Ways of Seeing*, that art should not be reserved (in both senses of the word) to the confines of the unoffensive and traditionally beautiful. To integrate whatever elements of reality into one's art — like real-life, no-holds-barred language — is okay.

In the visual arts, integrating objects from life obtains similar results. Sonic Youth's use of language and subject matter is like Haim Steinbach's assemblages of everyday objects. By taking something run-of-the-mill like shiny chrome garbage cans or Brooks Brothers suits and repositioning them into the world of art, Steinbach, with cynicism and more than a touch of wit, questions the validity of that art. In other words, his work, next to a more traditional sculpture by, say, Auguste Rodin, makes the viewer examine what makes both of them art (or good, or beautiful). Similarly, Moore's and Gordon's dry, almost-speaking voices, telling tales of real life in street language, next to a more traditionally musical voice (the examples are endless) makes the listener ponder just what good singing is, period. This phenomenon, of course, runs through a whole range of artists' work in a variety of media, from pop artists like Roy Lichtenstein (with his enlarged comics) and Andy Warhol (with Brillo pad boxes, Campbell's soup cans, and Marilyn Monroe silk screens) to David Mamet's real-life-dialogue plays to Philip Larkin's poetry in a collection like *High Windows*, where words like "fuck" are used to draw stark portraits of reality. Like the work of these artists, or of postmodern ones like Julian Schnabel or Jeff Koons, Sonic Youth's music goes beyond the traditional confines of its medium (like, say, guitars in tune) in the interest of self-expression. But what Sonic Youth does is broader than that: The band uses real-life language and lyrics to pull its music out of a distanced CD speaker and straight into its fans' lives.

For me, that discarding of the distinction between fancy refined art and real life (or, in alternative bands, between slickly produced pop fodder and the from-the-street punch of Sonic Youth), which is such an integral element of the work of a Warhol or a Koons or, to draw earlier examples, a Marcel Duchamp or a Man Ray, is, of course, one of the key components in an initial definition of postmodernism. This mixture of high and low is a recurring theme in Sonic Youth's work. If pop music has come to be equated with easy, sweet disposability and alternative music with something more credible, more complicated, and less immediate, then Sonic Youth's blending of pop with its distinctive, arty grunge is just that. This is shown by the "one-off" record the band recorded under the name Ciccone Youth (along with Mike Watt from FIREHOSE) (Ciccone as in Madonna Ciccone, the superstar's given name). The album, tauntingly titled *The Whitey Album* in a spoof of the Beatles' double album, features a cover of Madonna's "Into the Groove." The blend is also clear on the track "Madonna, Sean and Me" from the *Evol* album (which, incidentally, is also known as "Expressway to Yr Skull"). And as an artist like Warhol places icons like Jacqueline Kennedy Onassis and Elvis Presley in his work to comment on society, Sonic Youth has included references to everything from the Clarence Thomas Supreme Court hearings ("Youth Against Fascism") to Alfred Hitchcock films ("Shadow of a Doubt") to Karen Carpenter's anorexia ("Tunic (Song for Karen)") as a way of placing its work firmly in the land of TV news, urban street life, American culture-reality. The kitsch quality of Warhol's work is also mirrored in Gordon's and Moore's fashion sense, which mixes sixties hot pants and go-go boots with a sassy "fuck you" attitude, twisting sixties sex appeal into something undeniably nineties. And that tongue-in-cheek adaptation of kitsch elements from real life – both lyrically in songs like "Teen Age Riot" and "Tunic (Song for Karen)" and through their image – is, as Fredric Jameson mentions in his essay titled "The Cultural Logic of Late Capitalism" – a standard postmodern device. From postmodern architecture à la Robert Venturi's *Learning from Las Vegas* book to Warhol to what is probably the most obvious example, the work of sculptor Jeff Koons, who mixes commercial icons like Michael Jackson and Hummel figures with "high art" components like fine porcelain, the point is the same.

But Sonic Youth has gone farther than just commenting on pop icons – it has become the symbol itself for not "selling out" and changing sound or image or content. In fact, in the world of alternative music, its members themselves have become icons as individuals. Just as certain long-standing avant-gardists, like Jean-Luc Godard or Phillip Glass or even someone who bridges the conventionality gap like David Lynch, have become iconographic representatives of sticking to one's artistic guns, for having an adventurous artistic vision, or, from a more mainstream view, for being just plain weird, so has Sonic Youth. Having maintained a long career in the alternative realm, the band has a large audience by alternative standards. Although the Youth now have some of the superficial signs of "rock star" life – like a major-label deal with DGC, a major management company (Gold Mountain) – they have made no compromises. The band has stayed true to its initial goal of making music on its own terms. It has consistently built its core audience instead of alienating it.

For an alternative band, decisions like signing to a major label can have major repercussions with fans. In the early days of alternative music, there was an elitist distinction made by many fans between independently released music – credible, arty, adventurous, cool – and that which had major-label affiliation – blander, more commercial. Some bands were branded "sell-outs" merely by their signing a major-label deal. Yet Sonic Youth has maintained its sound and image while working within mainstream label systems. Certainly, there are other bands that have done the same thing. Hüsker Dü's signing to Warner Brothers in the mid-eighties set a precedent that was quickly followed by the likes of R.E.M., the Replacements, and a few years later, Nirvana when these bands affiliated with majors. But because Sonic Youth's "fuck-establishment" attitude is such a key part of its music, the band illustrates that an alternative group can sign to a major without losing its initial audience.

The images of Moore and Gordon, who are married, have also stretched into the realm of the symbolic. They have become the Sonny and Cher of the alternative realm: no-frills icons, almost anti-icons, who say to their fans that it's okay for married couples to look unconventional and wear cool clothes and play rock 'n' roll. Just as their music breaks the rules that say that music should sound in tune and songs should have tight structures, so the public face of their relationship – grungy husband and hipster-vixen wife – breaks the rules of a stereotypical marriage.

But just as this kind of blatant rule breaking is an omnipresent (and exciting) element of the Youth's sound, there is also a dark side to their music. There's always something sinister going on, whether or not it's literally explored in the song (like, say, the scenes of violent death in "Death Valley 69" or "100%"). There is an almost creepy quality, reinforced by the seemingly out-of-tune guitars, on tracks like "Swimsuit Issue," "Silver Rocket," and "Ghost Bitch." It's a kind of aural inclemence. Several of the band's album covers also imply that something's wrong. *Goo*'s cover is a stark cartoon of a sixties-era couple with the eerie caption, "I stole my sister's boyfriend. It was a whirlwind, heat and flash. Within a week we killed my parents and hit the road." The packaging of the *Dirty* album features stark color photographs of slightly deformed stuffed animals (by artist Mike Kelley); *Evol*'s cover is a photograph of a gnarling girl in a negligee – sort of a B-movie star gone psycho – with the band's name, the album title, and messy squiggles superimposed on top. Just as *Evol* is "love" backwards, the cover is everything sweet and pretty about love turned inside out – much like the music it surrounds. The suggestion is that modern life carries in it a similar apocalyptic warning of impending doom. That bleak threat permeates everything. It's the musical analogue of paintings by Jean Michel Basquiat or Antoni Tapies: an expression of the harshness of modern life affecting everything. It's certainly present in the work of Gerhard Richter, whose stark pieces, both called *Kerze*, are on the front and back covers of the band's 1988 double album, *Daydream Nation*, which is perhaps Sonic Youth's finest work to date. The threat of something bad about to happen is like the buildup soundtrack of a vintage Hitchcock film – what seems like background music heightens as if to clue you in as to what is in store. That's Sonic Youth's constant backdrop. But it's that grim quality, the expression of the confusion of modern life, that makes Sonic Youth's noise and inversion of musical rules seem not only natural but downright necessary.

The problems that accompany the depression and cynicism of modern-day life, including homelessness, AIDS, and impersonal violence, are part of the lives of both the Youth and their fans. That tension gives the band's music a sometimes frightening bite. Voices/ guitars/drums explode almost uncontrollably in a "we're-bursting" way, as if that music is the only means of escape. And for fans who feel trapped in their adolescent lives or small towns or shitty New York apartments or unemployed situations, listening to Sonic Youth's music, with its volume and loose constructions, its eerie guitar twists and battle-cry drums, delivers that escape. The metaphorical connection between the tension in the music and in their lives even further intensifies the, well, intensity of both.

Some of the American guitar bands the Youth has influenced equally instill their music with a sense of grim surroundings, even if those surroundings are the virtual inverse of New York. Case in point: Nirvana, who opened for Sonic Youth before its "Teen Spirit" rise to fame. The Sonic Youth's dark vision is to urban New York what Nirvana's is to middle America. The latter band's sound, along with that of the other bands that round out this chapter's discussion, has been labeled "the Seattle sound" because the majority of bands which realize it began their recording careers on SubPop records, an independent label based in Seattle. But to lump these bands together and imply that their strongest link is the feel and experience of life in Seattle is just plain wrong. The real point is that while a band like the Fall reeks of its Manchester home, Nirvana expresses the anger and boredom and depression of living in one of a thousand American towns. And incidentally, to be precise, Nirvana's members are not from Seattle but a smaller town called Aberdeen in Washington. Kids long to escape but don't know exactly how. To me, that's why Nirvana has sold the millions of records it has. Its get-me-out-of-here fury, both musical and lyrical, resonates deeply within listeners from many different places. The way I see it, Nirvana and country star Garth Brooks and John Cougar Mellencamp and *Born to Run*–era Bruce Springsteen offer precisely the same thing: an expression of real life based not in the customary American media capitals of New York and Los Angeles, but in no-frills U.S.A. And for all different sorts of people who want an antidote to the slickness of most of what comes out of those capitals, each of those artists delivers in a different way.

Nevertheless, Nirvana couldn't have sold seven million records by merely expressing a middle-American ethic. In my view, the band's huge success essentially has to do with two elements. First, when the recession started to snowball in America and across so much of the world in the second half of 1991, listeners began to long for something equal parts "cut-the-bullshit" un-slick and "we're-fed-up" angry. That mixture is certainly part of all the tracks on Nirvana's *Nevermind* album, which resonates with all the tracks on the Sex Pistols' *Never Mind the Bollocks, Here's the Sex Pistols* from 1977 unemployment-dirged England. Second, underneath the raw edges of a punked-out Rod Stewart voice, Nirvana writes classic, stick-in-your-head, get-them-on-the-first-listen pop tunes. The "Smells Like Teen Spirit" single exemplifies that talent. The band intensifies and brutalizes those tunes with its own qualities: namely, drummer Dave Grohl's threatening, rocket-bursting-off-his-drumstool drumming, bass player Chris Novoselic's manic pulse, and lead singer Kurt Cobain's eerie, get-me-out-of-here voice. These are the nuances that give Nirvana's music its postmodern stamp. Nirvana's perversion of self-written sweet pop songs to speak to its audience in its own language is a gesture similar to Andy Warhol's when he painted portraits of Campbell's soup cans.

Those layers of volume and biting guitars that Nirvana packs onto their songs like a chef piling more cheese onto a hearty lasagne have led some critics to label the band, along with the ones who've gained popularity in their wake, "grunge bands." It's a valid enough description — those listen-up layers are a common component in the work of Nirvana, Afghan Whigs, Pearl Jam, Soundgarden, Mudhoney, and so on — except it's just too simple. What these bands really represent is the assimilation of top-40 radio pop song accessibility, the roar of metal, the fuck-the-mainstream attitude of punk, and the apathetic disengagement of being stuck in a situation from which you want out. There's no one catchphrase or label that can capture all these overriding influences of so many of the kids who are into Nirvana. And, let's face it, those feelings of dissatisfaction and entrapment are pretty much a given at a certain age — the joys of adolescence. Nirvana just actualizes them sonically, with or without lyrics.

In fact, the lyrics are not really where the bottom-line force of the band comes from. When the single "Smells Like Teen Spirit" was on the charts in America and Europe, most fans only deciphered snippets of lyrics: notably, "Hello, hello, hello" repeated over and over again, becoming almost a subliminal chant. This device was also used in lines like: "You're so good for me/you destroy me" and the "Nevers" in Marguerite Duras's "Hiroshima Mon Amour." In both cases, the would-be mantras are drummed in so that the individual words lose their meaning, becoming like a tribal incantation or an ambulance siren. The siren analogy more strictly applies to the music itself. The band's booming guitars—propelled by Grohl's spot-on bang and Cobain's emergency voice, as bolting and as urgent as a clanging fire alarm—are as desperate as a suicidal man on a window ledge—they're filled with this almost tangible "get-me-out-of-here" force. The sound portends doom—as even the first pulsating bars of "Teen Spirit" demonstrate—with an energy that is different from Sonic Youth's but equally intense.

And that's just the music. My take on music with that kind of sonic surge, presented with clarity, is that even if the band was garbling in baby talk, its music would roar. For example, *Nevermind* (1991), well produced with a decent budget, has a wide-eyed force that its predecessor, *"Bleach"* (1989), recorded for $600, only hints at. Although I don't intend to minimize the substance of lyrics by the Sex Pistols or the Clash or even Nirvana, the vocal punch of those bands comes more from the open-sore rawness of their lead singers and their in-your-face charisma than from the initial impact of their lyrics. Lead singers Johnny Rotten, Joe Strummer, Mick Jones, and Kurt Cobain are just so intensely riveting that their voices, at least to me, are fulfilling enough. Nirvana's "we're-trapped" aesthetic is reinforced by the repeated refrain of "No, I don't have a gun" in "Come as You Are" or "Smell Like Teen Spirit"'s "I feel stupid, and contagious/here we are now, entertain us." But the punch of the music, even when you can't understand the words, lies more in its sound than in its textual meaning.

The obtuse titles of the band's songs—"Territorial Pissings," "Breed," and "Lithium" on *Nevermind*, and "Sifting" and "Blew" on *"Bleach"*—is the main focus. This prioritization of sound over lyrics brings up a key issue: If the underlying force behind the music of Nirvana—and My Bloody Valentine and Sonic Youth and so many of the other bands discussed in this book—is the confusion of modern life, then those gauzy song titles are the equivalent of the miasma bands' blurring of musical details. It's as if even a more conventional song title would be equally hard to pinpoint in a world where it's hard to figure out "what things mean," "what to do," "what is right and wrong." For these bands, life is confusing and, more often than not, unintelligible. Expressing that in titles or enigmatic lyrics seems natural.

The violent confusion of Nirvana's fans' world – a world of boredom and TV burnout and kids looking for a way out – is reflected in their main mode of dance, called "moshing." Moshing is the nineties version of slam dancing. It involves kids pounding into each other. It encourages kids to "stagedive" – to climb up on the stage and bound onto the shoulders of the audience. At the front of the standing-audience area at these gigs, there's a "mosh pit": an area where kids throw themselves at each other, run into each other, slam up against each other. More often than not, a handful of kids will climb onto the shoulders of the audience closest to the stage and literally get passed along by a horde of kids with their arms raised. From above, it looks like a sick take on a game of volleyball; for the audience, it feels more like war – or a triage line in an army hospital. For these kids, moshing releases aggressions in a manner that is somewhat detached from the music, but still driven by its volume, growl, and pounded-out pace. It's the same release as on a basketball court, as in front of a pinball machine, as on a football field. Maybe some of these kids would release that aggression through violence. Moshing puts parameters around physical violence but sneaks in just enough of it to let kids get their anger out. Just as punk rock and so many of the alternative movements that have followed it encourage a breakdown of the distinction between rock star performer and average fan, so stagediving unifies musician and audience, allowing the latter to smash through the invisible wall at the stage's front. For a moment, fans are in the spotlight, participating in an active way with the band. Compare this interaction with, say, sitting in a plush, upholstered seat at the opera, and you've captured some of the energy of these bands live. With an audience gnarled into a physical group frenzy, it's the difference between watching a baseball game on TV and participating stretched out on third base.

Again, unless you're in a grimy rock club, the activity of intentionally rebounding off fellow audience members and jumping onto and off of the stage mid-song may seem strange, but as accompaniment to the soundtrack-to-the-apocalypse that is Nirvana, it makes complete sense. Furthermore, if part of adolescent angst is longing to be part of something, defining yourself in groups beyond the family unit, even replacing the family unit, as is natural for of latch-kids and members of dysfunctional or single-parent families, the interreliance of moshing gives kids, if only for the hour and a half or so length of a band's set, that feeling of community. For some kids, gangs can offer a similar release of tension and adolescent energy. For alternative fans, the release is nonviolent and limited by the bounds of a gig.

Of course, part of identifying oneself as a member of a community is looking like the other members of that community. Just as male and female miasma fans dress the same, in loose t-shirts and jeans, and grebo fans scruff themselves into outfits of lived-in dirt-fashion, fans of American guitar bands have a specific look. De rigueur fashions for grunge fans include Doctor Marten boots – big, clunky, unisex shoes, somewhere between work boots and orthopedic shoes, almost anti-fashion in their utilitarianism – and, over a t-shirt (often emblazoned with the name of a cool band), a lumberjack shirt – sometimes tied around one's waist like a backwards apron, often worn with the sleeves torn off, leaving frayed threads like an obtuse metaphor of decaying America. The look is humble, accessible, shared by fans and stars. There's no image or facade or affluence about it. It's a sturdy look that seems all too appropriate for kids coping with a recession, a depleted ozone layer, and the threat of AIDS. If the glitz of Michael Jackson made sense in the wealthy eighties, then the austerity and traditionalism-gone-bad of a ripped work shirt and last-forever boots is the right look for the early nineties. If the noise and fuck-you anger of grunge parallels punk, so the battered clothes represent (whether consciously or not) a larger depression. And, like the mods and skinheads and two-tone boys in England in the early eighties, along with a couple of generations of heavy metal fans, these fans' look gives them a sense of identity as part of a group of like-minded fans who embody specific ideologies.

Of course, after *Nevermind*'s worldwide success in 1991 and 1992, designer versions of grunge fashion were seen on runways and in fashion shows. Lumberjack shirts were all of a sudden being worn by rappers and Madonna and anyone else who jumped on the trend-of-the-month bandwagon. The sociological coherence of the look diffused; its impact had become so unavoidable among an ever-expanding bunch of grunge fans that its appeal expanded beyond its initial demographic. But grunge fans' initial impulse toward these clothes – cheap, utilitarian, functional, long-lasting, unisex – has little to do with fashion or commerce. If anything, these clothes are anti-fashion – frill-free for a no-frills soundtrack reflecting stark, depressing lives. And so fashion magazines and designers found anti-glitzy, pixie-faced models, like Kate Moss and Kristen McMenamy:

as much the visual antithesis of supercoiffed supermodels like Cindy Crawford as Nirvana is the antithesis of Madonna.

If Sonic Youth's Moore and Gordon have become anti-icons, so have the members of Nirvana in the wake of their success. All three members let fans know that a band could be on a major label, maintain the gruff bite of its original charm, and still hit the charts. The message also is that no one has to conform to expectations. In Nirvana's case, not conforming meant there was no need to tone down raw vocals, use intelligible song titles, or clean Cobain's ragamuffin hair. Soon after the release and explosion of *Nevermind*, Cobain began dating Courtney Love, the lead singer of Hole, and so became labeled by some critics as half of the "Sid and Nancy" of the Seattle scene, referring to Sex Pistol Sid Vicious and his girlfriend Nancy Spungen and their drug-obsessed, grim, but bound-at-the-hip relationship. Once again, the message is anti-conformist: Love and Cobain, with ratty hair and hand-me-down clothes and nowhere looks, are as valid a couple as a more traditional one. So, just as Cobain's makes us question musical conventions with his anti-singing and his subversion of pop songs with mangled guitars and heart-attack drums, so he and his now-wife Love twist the conventional image of a happy couple and make us question the validity of that conventional image as well. A *Vanity Fair* profile of them described alleged drug use, in particular during Love's pregnancy. Like Robert Mapplethorpe's mid-seventies black-and-white photographs of sadomasochistic scenes, the couples' image is brutal, angry, controversial, thought provoking, and contradicts past aesthetics without ever needing to articulate that conflict.

Small and scruffy, with a voice like twigs crushing underneath a workman's boot, Cobain is hardly the clean, too-pretty, sparkling frontman you'd think of as a sex symbol. Obviously, Cobain as frontman/star/poster boy is an alternative image. I mean, compare Cobain's scrawny snarl to, say, Tom Cruise's gleam, and the idea of Cobain-as-pinup seems almost absurd.

But, if you examine what the band is about (and see Nirvana live, and really listen to the band's records), to pull Cobain to the forefront is more a media exploit than an inherent quality of the band. Nirvana is unquestionably the sum of its three very involved parts. Which is not to say that all Seattle/grunge/whatever-you-want-to-call-them bands of this school necessarily have that anti–focal point, populist ethic. With Soundgarden, for example, all audience eyes lead to hunky lead singer Chris Cornell. But Nirvana feels like a community of three democratic members—which offers an added appeal for fans who dress, dance, and act like their fellow fans and so form a community themselves.

In the wake of Nirvana's huge international success, record companies clamored to release and sign bands that they felt fit into Nirvana's musical realm and so might approach its success. Some of these bands, like the Afghan Whigs, have enough of their own musical chutzpah to hint at some long-term potential. Others do not. Pearl Jam, for example, may continue selling but, on its album *Ten* (which climbed the charts post-Nirvana), seems like a bland, scattered combination of grunge and Led Zeppelin. Bands like Alice in Chains blend Black Sabbath with grunge for similarly flat results. But these bands are not imitators so much as similarly minded musicians expressing something that they have in common: a growling discontent with status-quo pop, status-quo metal, status-quo life—a bursted-out feeling of wanting to escape. Despite all they have in common, though, many of the bands have different musical antecedents: Soundgarden and Alice in Chains have clear Black Sabbath roots, Pearl Jam has a similarly seventies-based sound, and Mudhoney, featuring former members of Green River, a seminal Seattle alternative band, are as pop-around-grunge–based as Nirvana.

Some of the bands whose records have appeared in Nirvana's wake, like Helmet and Quicksand, are, to my ears, more about intrusive energy than inherent musicality. Like a Jackson Pollock painting, they're about frazzle and angst, but they hit you abstractly instead of with "I've-experienced-that" specificity. That fury is hard to capture in the often sterile setting of a recording studio or music video set, and so these bands' live shows are the way to get what they're about. To fully understand it, this music must be seen and heard live, which gives it a disturbingly ephemeral quality: It's as if American grunge music is a tape that is so intense it's guaranteed to self-destruct. And because these bands are so much about live energy, which is inherently based in the present, it's hard to imagine, say, sounding particularly relevant in five years' time.

A few of the more interesting bands of the post-Nirvana wave twist conventions in a way similar to the way Nirvana does but by adding their own musical elements in a different ratio from Nirvana's. Mudhoney, for example, pushes its jukebox-ready pop songs right up front. On albums like *Every Good Boy Deserves Fudge* (which came out on SubPop in 1991) and its self-titled debut album (also on SubPop, from 1989), the band is certainly as loud/fedback/metal-meets-punk-meets-Northwestern-American-boredom-ed as Nirvana, but Nirvana's open-sore anger is replaced by a poppier focus. Since Nirvana's success, Mudhoney has signed to Warner Brothers Records.

The Afghan Whigs, who are often lumped in with Seattle bands because their records have come out on SubPop, aren't actually from Seattle but from Cincinnati, Ohio. Although they seem bored with their surroundings, they boom on a stage, and their music has more depth — and influences beyond punk — than that of many of their contemporaries. In particular, their 1992 album, *Congregation*, mixes hard punk-based guitar pound with elements of mainstream pop, rock, and even jazz. Their music is less biting than Nirvana's, but, in the long run, sounds less "of the moment" and more long-term listenable. As with so many alternative bands, just when you expect it to be conventional/predictable, as on a good-from-the-first-listen track like "Turn on the Water," the voice fucks up, the guitar goes spastic, the drums beat with more fury than they're supposed to. In other words, what could be conventional is made alternative.

Perhaps the clearest example of that kind of twist is the Whigs' marvelous version of Diana Ross and the Supremes' "My World Is Empty Without You," which is the B-side of the band's "Conjure Me" single, also taken from the *Congregation* album. It begins with a near-normal beat, pounded as hard as a tribal war drum instead of the backbeat to a cool pop ditty. A snake-charmer guitar is introduced after the first couple bars, which keeps being repeated again and again, ominously, throughout the song, like the leitmotif of, say, the Peer Gynt theme in the movie *M*. Lead singer Greg Dulli's voice is really what does it, though. He's literally wailing, seemingly consumed with agony and tears and despair. If you want to get literal about things, it's soul music, plain and simple. And, of course, for anyone who's ever felt lonely or dumped, it's Dulli as everyman, his crackling warble not only enabling but actually compelling listeners to empathize.

Certainly, his yelp is in sharp contrast to the velvet-smooth gleam of Diana Ross's original version. That contrast is equally pronounced on the band's sinister, desperate cover of "Come See About Me" on its *Uptown Avondale* EP, which came out in 1992. But the intensity or punch does not end with Dulli's voice. Where the sixties original inserts shmaltzy sixties details, as dated now as a go-go mini-dress, the Whigs take cocktail lounge guitars and plunge them in feedback — the listener, like the singer, is jolted, headached, flipped out. Live, lead singer Dulli often lets his guitar simply hang and sullenly lights a cigarette during the song, like a Twilight Zoned classic torch singer. Where the Supremes' original has a deep, booming bass line, the Whigs plug in that wavy guitar line, a wiry shock over a deep throb. Notably, a couple of the original's pop conventions — the "ooh babe" background verse vocals, the raised octaves at the end — are left in.

Maybe it seems microscoped-out to go into such great depth about just one song, let alone a B-side, yet the Whigs' take on "My World Is Empty Without You" technically and musically embodies alternative music. The passion, the assertiveness, and the frustration provide a catharsis to the listener that is an alternative to the repressed gloss of more mainstream pop music. The rawness of that Afghan Whigs cut is captured by having recorded on only eight tracks (music is recorded on different tracks — i.e., one for drums, one for vocals, etc. — and then combined; most albums are recorded on twenty-four or forty-eight tracks; eight tracks is primitive even by demo standards).

Following their two albums on SubPop — and Nirvana's success — the Afghan Whigs signed to Elektra amidst offers from several major labels. By then (late 1992/early 1993), Nirvana, without Michael Jackson artifice, had proved that the intensity and purity of a band like the Whigs could also have sales appeal. But before even entering the studio to record that first major-label release, the band recorded more raw, anguished versions of classic pop songs, like the Supremes' "Come See About Me," sung as a near-suicidal ultimatum, and a pounded-out take on Freda Payne's "Band of Gold," which are as un-slicked and as personalized as their version of "My World Is Empty Without You."

Post-Nirvana, or, more correctly, post-Nirvana-sales, major labels scrambled to sign what they felt might best capitalize on the floodgates the band opened. Seattle's Soundgarden, which is more firmly based in a metal tradition and features Led Zeppelin-esque guitars, was already signed to major A&M. Pearl Jam, whose Epic debut picked up Nirvana's momentum and sold extremely well, was also signed before the floodgates opened. But soon to follow *Nevermind*'s climb to the top were major-label signings of grunge bands Mudhoney, the Afghan Whigs, the Melvins (whose debut Atlantic album was produced by none other than Nirvana's Kurt Cobain), Paw, Helmet, Quicksand and the list goes on and on. Spin-off projects, like Temple of the Dog, featuring members of Soundgarden and Mother Love Bone, were rereleased. Since grunge was selling, major labels began to co-opt a thriving indie scene. Since they were selling records and t-shirts and concert tickets, these bands began to attract major-league managers, booking agents, and lawyers. They began to play bigger halls. A film, *Singles*, set in Seattle and filled with a soundtrack by bands like Mudhoney, Soundgarden, and Pearl Jam, came out in September 1992.

But it's not just about marketing. For me, this school of American guitar bands speaks to something – and from someplace – that is the eighties and nineties American equivalent of punk – anger and boredom and a need to get out. And as so many of the problems that seem to create a fertile breeding ground for these bands – from the microscope-view of a disengaged teenager cutting school to grab a smoke with his friends to the larger view of a decreasing ozone layer and unemployment – show no signs of going away, the music seems to have a long-term relevance. Sure, there's a transience to it, since it's best heard live-and-fleeting, but on a sociological level, "grunge" bands speak to a basic need for kids to have no-bullshit music to which they can relate. But as is the wont of the music industry, labels tend to jump onto bandwagons, over-sign bands in a certain genre, and then hop off onto something else. From post–Tracy Chapman folkies to post-Madonna bop-divas, it inevitably seems to happen. And so the spotlight slips off alternative American guitar bands onto something else.

Which, because theirs is a music of anti-hype, anti-manufacture, anti-standard-music, would mean that these bands would have to operate outside of mainstream systems like major labels and *Rolling Stone* and within the alternative realm in which they began. Which, given what they're doing musically and ideologically, might be more appropriate, anyway. Bands like Sonic Youth and Dinosaur Jr. sound as though they're making exactly the sounds they want to make without answering to anyone. For those two bands, who established large fan bases before signing to a major, calling the shots is no problem. But it might be for a younger band in the Nirvana aftertow. So "fuck-establishment" music probably has a more secure home in a "fuck-establishment" medium – that is, on an independent label that won't complain if the music isn't commercial or trendy or radio-friendly. But whether it's released on a major or on an indie, the important thing is that this music, which is such a vivid expression of youthful frustration, boredom, and rage, comes out period.

GREBO
FIVE
BANDS

"Grebo" is an alien word to Americans—to the British it means sludgy, messy, stick-on-your-hands like molasses dirt. In other words, grunge. As bands like Nirvana represent American grunge—lazy, disinterested, disengaged kids—there is a school of British bands that exude an equally intense energy and, in some ways, an equally dark vibe. The label some journalists, predominantly in England, have given them is "grebo bands." While they sound and look different from American grunge bands, their escape-from-boredom impetus is essentially the same. Except that, while there's a darkness to what a band like Nirvana does, the grebos incorporate humor into their release-for-escape.

The key bands of this movement—Mega City Four (the band from which the movement really hatched), Ned's Atomic Dustbin, the Wonder Stuff, Pop Will Eat Itself, Senseless Things—all pound with a booming crisis-ed roar. But while bands like Dinosaur Jr. feature an emphatic pound that is heavy and somber, the pulse of grebo music is filled with youth and vitality and spirit. Grebo is about a fifteen-year-old kid feeling trapped, yet who wants to bolt out and explore life instead of ending it. If Nirvana is an angry kid pounding a punching bag, Mega City Four is a revved-up kid dancing in front of his bathroom mirror, dreaming of how his life could be better and free.

Grebo bands are fueled by a nonstop, sweet, buoyant churn — like a puppy zealously fetching sticks for its owner. Or, more appropriately, like a teenager's hormones, overbuzzed, overactive, zooming about with nowhere to go. While the precursor for bands like Nirvana is punk, grebos add a heavy pop sensibility. The focus is not so much on the wail of the guitar but rather the overall boom of the band as a whole. And while bands like the Jam and the Clash have influenced the grebos, it is for their captivating tunes played through too-fast guitars rather than for their political stance. Some of the bands, like the Wonder Stuff and the Levellers, use celtic touches like fiddles and Irish-based harmonies. Other, like Pop Will Eat Itself, blend dance beats into the music. Which is not to imply slick musical sophistication or even decided "let's-add-these-bits-together" thought — grebo bands are about no-frills spontaneity, about an almost folksy all-join-in ethic.

Grebo can be seen as the British version of grunge — a ferociously powered, nonstop reaction against slick, refined, restrained top-40 music. Its exploding-soda-can power is key — that's part of what distinguishes the anti–top-40 reaction of grebos from the softer response of art bands or miasma bands. I would argue that it's just one British version of grunge — if grunge is fed-up kids escaping through edged-out music, then the miasma bands and feedback bands certainly fulfill those credentials as well. But there's an extra link between grebo and grunge — it has to do with image (or lack of it) and with kids' devotion.

That die-hard fandom is most apparent in England, where fans of some of these bands follow their tours across the country, like updated Deadheads. But that alliance doesn't stop with mere attendance: Grebo fans put their money where their mouths are. Certainly, it's become a given in rock 'n' roll — basically, because there's money to be made at it — that fans buy and wear t-shirts at gigs. In the case of the grebo bands, that merchandising has had almost exaggerated importance. Before signing their major-label deal with Sony worldwide, Ned's Atomic Dustbin subsidized its touring with sales of numerous styles of t-shirts, shorts, caps, and basically anything the band could come up with to sell. After its record deal was signed, the band continued to churn out t-shirts, constantly changing the designs to satisfy fans. Other grebo bands, like the Levellers and Carter the Unstoppable Sex Machine, have done the same. The grebo bands have based their looks around the street styles of skate punks and rap kids, and have combined their own mix of clashing fashion statements. And frequently, grebo kids base *their* looks around merchandised t-shirts – plastered with favorite bands' names – to broadcast their alliances.

But the way grebo bands and their fans dress is about more than t-shirts. The potluck nuances of the look parallel what's going on in the music. The musical jumble varies from band to band, but what grebos have in common is an attitude of pulling together different elements that often represent some alliance or ideological stance (i.e., Scottish tartans, Rastafarian dreadlocks). By juxtaposing these components in a specific way, the bands twist the semiotic meaning of those clothes and make them their own. In other words, their dress parallels what their music does – what so many alternative bands do – exactly. For example, the members of Ned's Atomic Dustbin – five pimply kids from the depressed West Midlands district of England – scruff their hair into matted dreadlocks traditionally worn by Rastafarians. Juxtaposed against that hairdo are surfer shorts and baggy t-shirts, often emblazoned with the name of a cool band. It's a hodgepodge blend – clean white Brit boys, ratty hair, loose clothes that look more suited to either a California beachcomber or a kid-rapper like one of the members of Kris Kross. But it seems thoroughly appropriate with the band's music, a pandemonious mixture of classic pop tunes, chunky guitar playing, and a whole mess of energy. It's no wonder some British journalists have dubbed the grebo movement "crusty," since its fans, more often than not, seem to be encrusted in a layer of grime.

Other grebo bands also tie together otherwise clashing styles, like Jesus Jones's backwards baseball caps (a rap fashion) and surfer shorts and Miles Hunt's (the Wonder Stuff's lead singer) long hair and earring paired with a traditional men's kilt. Sometimes it looks almost silly – but, then again, there's an element of silliness in what grebo bands do musically. Their look may be considerably cleaner, but it still demonstrates a mix of mismatched elements.

The "grebo label" describes the behavior of these bands and their fans as much as it does the music. While a mainstream artist might have a hairstylist and be clean around the edges, bands like Mega City Four and Ned's Atomic Dustbin revel in the mud on their boots and their cacophonous hair. It's like each bit of grime is a war medal for gigs played or outdoor music festivals attended. Again, the "crusty" label is an appropriate and evocative one. For fans, to be able to wallow in that unkempt state is to be free—it's the same feeling a nine-year-old has when, after being told to wash behind his ears, he instead rolls around in the mud with friends. And, once again, what fan groups are about is selecting elements—behavioral, fashion-wise—that might seem inappropriate outside that group but that they can use to identify themselves on the inside. This phenomenon isn't limited to grebo fans. It works for punks and skinheads and mod fans and loads of others, although the manifestations are different in terms of fashion and behavior. Just as these musicians take the pop conventions and contort them, they take conventional clothes and soil them, rip them, and wear them out as a fashion equivalent to what they're doing musically.

The grebos' hodgepodge of different fashion elements—baseball caps, surfer shorts, Doc Martens, dreadlocks—is consonant with a similar collection of seemingly disparate elements in the music. For alternative music fans, as well as for the musicians themselves, life means assimilating a barrage of influences—the invasive media, almost surreal political changes in so many parts of the world, the alarming decay of the ozone layer and the rain forests. For some musicians, like those in My Bloody Valentine, music is a drug-like catharsis; for others, like those in the Wedding Present and Dinosaur Jr., music is a shake-it-out-of-you release. For the grebos, music is the empowering assimilation of all the cacophonous stimuli, a juxtaposition of different sounds, spliced together almost like sound bites, like the evening news. More specifically, grebo music makes fun of—and has fun with—this evening-news pileup. Seemingly mismatched clothing—pulling together lots of different, would-be disparate elements—parallels the grebos' musical merging.

To that end, many grebo bands integrate sampling—of snippets of dialogue and language as well as of beats—into their songs. Jesus Jones, a band that I lump in with the grebos even though it has burst beyond that base, exemplifies this technique. On the band's first album, *Liquidizer*, it samples everything from dance music to a Bulgarian Women's choir. In fact, the title refers to that jumbled mix. Ned's

Atomic Dustbin and Pop Will Eat Itself also use samples. A band like the Wonder Stuff has a live violinist to add that unexpected musical mix live. The common ground of the grebos, for me, is still the musical churn, like rushing train wheels underneath. Their music has the nonstop force of a day-long thunderstorm, pounding incessantly. Basically, it's a British reading of the seethed gurgle that is the musical base for Hüsker Dü's records. This force is what makes tracks like Mega City Four's "Who Cares" or Ned's Atomic Dustbin's "Happy" definitively alternative; it adds a palpable urgency to these bands' music.

The roots of that grebo churn are in Mega City Four, a band formed in 1988 by four normal guys from Farnborough in northern England. They built their audience by touring virtually nonstop, beginning locally and then driving as far as they could go. These scruffy guys with seemingly dirty clothes and a lead singer with near-dreadlocks and a pierced nose look more like fans than musicians. And that's precisely the point: If punk dismissed the distinction between glitzy rock star and lowly fan, the Megas (as their fans call them) celebrate the resultant similarities, exaggerate them, and so take the fans' sense of fitting in to a group of like-minded people one step further. Their concentration on their live show stresses this point: The band is as much about live energy as music, as much about no-frills, empathize-with-them visuals as about songs. And Megas gigs—like those of any band with such a clear image (or anti-image), look, etc.—are as much a meeting place for similarly minded kids as a school dance or a church social. And if Nirvana gigs or Wedding Present gigs are a meeting place for the dropouts, Megas gigs are for dropouts with a sense of humor.

In an age when music videos, and the pretense they often include, are a given for bands, there's a reactionary aspect to the Megas'—and all grebo bands'—concentration on live gigs. The spontaneity and community of a gig—versus the rehearsed, in-your-house-sitting-on-the-sofa music video ethic—works against the mainstream norm as much as vinyl seven-inch singles in an age of CDs do. If a lipsynching dance number on MTV by, say, Paula Abdul is the establishment, then the Megas' pure, bombastic live show is anti-establishment with a capital A. Certainly, this potent energy parallels that of the Sex Pistols, the Clash, hell, for that matter, Elvis Presley. For the grebos in the late eighties/early nineties, it expresses rebellion with as much venom as a vintage punk rock lyric, whether or not you understand any of the words. The grebo movement is propelled by just so many bopping kids, eager to believe in something. Instead of buying into a specific ideology or religion, they align themselves with a bunch of musicians who perform without a speck of artificiality, covered in grime. The grebo ethic is about a cleansing outburst of energy; it offers fans a release for their aggressions in a nonviolent and frequently ebullient way. And that bombastic power is clearest live.

It's worth examining the work of Mega City Four to see this energy in action. The band is equal parts super-urgent guitar and the strain-vocals of lead singer Wiz, who, apparently pushing too-hard, almost out of breath, bursts to get each line out. If Kurt Cobain from Nirvana is everyman's voice, Wiz is every teenager's. Teens feel trapped, rebel against some abstract but extra-vivid wall, try to knock that wall down with volume and rage. Wiz encapsulates that energy on stage even before he opens his mouth – and somehow evokes some of the fun of adolescence as well. In a sense, the band's music, even on record, is more about the band's impossible-to-avoid energy than specific songs. The albums play more like complete units than mere collections. This is even true of 1991's *Terribly Sorry Bob* LP (available as a British import on Decoy), which is actually a compilation of the band's early singles. Nevertheless, tracks like "Start" and "January," from the *Tranzophobia* album, explode into a pumped-up onslaught of guitars and drums after the first few bars. "Static Interference" and "Messenger," off the *Who Cares Wins* LP, are too fast, too intense, a race to squeeze as much energy into a three-minute pop song as possible. "Miles Apart" and "Severance," featured on *Terribly Sorry Bob*, and "Clown" and "What's Up" (from 1992's *Sebastopol Road* LP) exemplify what the band is about: a hammered-out punch that demands to be heard.

Again, for the Megas, as for many other grebo bands, that punch is more exuberant than pissed off. If music that is charged up is, in some people's minds, intrinsically aggressive (because it's just too fast, too spastic, like a chicken running around with its head cut off), then the Megas' music can be seen as such. But frankly, that's missing the point. Instead of nihilism, what the Megas preach is optimism. By creating a specific sound – as well as the look and attitude that go along with that sound – the band invites fans to an oasis where they belong. It's no coincidence, then, that the bulk of the "kids" who listen to the bands and go from gig to gig are just that – kids. Their music offers a parent-less, restrictionless release; it's as sweat-it-out charged as a basketball game in a schoolyard, as sweat-it-out cathartic as a hot, hot bath.

The almost excessive mile-a-minute vigor of the Megas—as impelling as a team coach standing behind a player's back chanting "faster, faster"—is echoed by many grebo bands, such as Carter the Unstoppable Sex Machine, the Wonder Stuff, and perhaps most intensely, Ned's Atomic Dustbin. The Neds are essentially kids themselves—when their first import-only album, *Bite*, came out, its members were still teenagers. And so the band combines the pulse of the Megas with its own empathize-along youthful stance. Both bands are a lot about pace and defining each song as their own within the first few bars—and so each has a distinctive sound. Building on the Megas' potent base, the Neds add an almost adolescent impatience, along with a skill for writing musical hooks that stick in your head. This is clear (whether you like it or not) on tracks like "Grey Cell Green" and "Happy." If the miasmics subvert traditional pop songs by blurring their edges, and American and British guitar bands do the same with extra-loud guitars ripping over the tune, then the Neds use that Mega-pound as their means to the same end.

As I've said before, the bursting-out power of the grebo bands is reminiscent, to me, of the frazzed-out energy of a teenage kid locked in a bedroom, dying to get out, rebelling against some abstract force as well as against parents, status quo, etc. In fact, many of these bands, like the Megas, the Neds, and Jesus Jones, have a tendency to pound their shaggy-haired heads during guitar licks at gigs—as if they're just bursting, about to explode, needing to release that extra jolt of emotional zeitgeist lest they pop. The Neds capture this energy more vividly than their contemporaries, possibly because the band members are so young that they are still actually riddled with some of that angst. Lyrically, on songs like "What Gives My Son?" and "Less than Useful," the band deals with adults' lack of understanding of their kids. And so, Ned's Atomic Dustbin fans can revel in music that is theirs, that expresses their issues. The Neds parallel the Who circa "My Generation" or the early Clash: The band expresses adolescent boredom and anger through both the jolted sound of its music and the personal nature of its lyrics. While they're not necessarily confessional, those lyrics are certainly rooted in the band members' own language and overall experiences; as they sing in *God Fodder*'s "What Gives My Son?": "Far be it from me to say you're brain dead/it might help if you get your ass out of bed."

The fact that the band's members are not much older than their

Quintessential grebo: Ned's Atomic Dustbin

fans is relevant. Like the members of the Senseless Things and EMF, the Neds have signed to major labels, made records, and toured around the world by the age of twenty and just under. If one of punk's messages was that anyone off the street—young, average, unmusical, ugly—could be in a band, that's grebo bands' message as well. The fact that band members look, act, and dress like their fans drives that message home. And, I should point out, this expression of the validity of young people's art was the motivation behind French New Wave Cinema, New German Cinema, and many other artistic movements.

The Neds' song titles and lyrics also represent a cynicism about some of the "givens" of modern life. One song is called "Kill Your Television." Another, "Grey Cell Green," questions the individual's role in a world of in-it-for-a-buck greed: "The grey cell's green only if the green sells grey." Songs like "Cut Up" and "Your Complex" are accusatory, you-don't-understand songs. "I know better/don't go telling me it's gone wrong," from "Your Complex," is a confrontational couplet. So is "You don't seem nothing like my friend" in "Nothing Like." It's no wonder that the band attracts hordes of kids—the members express their concerns in their own language, dress like their fans, and look like their fans. If mainstream rock is *Vogue* magazine, the Neds are *Sassy*.

It's worth pointing out that whereas bands like Mega City Four and the Senseless Things have had the bulk of their success in England, the Neds have done extremely well in America. Although the band's first album, *Bite*, which came out on the independent Chapter 22 label in England, was never released in America, their second, *God Fodder*, did extremely well in terms of sales and college and commercial alternative airplay in America. The band's next worldwide release, *Are You Normal?*, didn't sell quite as well but still got plenty of U.S. radio play. Aside from the vast amount of marketing, money, and tour support that Columbia Records used to help make it happen, I attribute this success to several key elements of the band's overall presentation.

First, the band writes classic, charmer pop songs—although those songs are processed through driving guitars, and so pop along faster than you might expect. This, of course, in my view is why Nirvana's "Smells Like Teen Spirit" succeeded as well: So-called alternative artists can break beyond that realm via a quality song, plain and simple.

Second, the adolescent rage of the band's music is universal. It defies nationality or cultural specificity. It is something that every teenager goes through. And although the band addresses issues of adolescence in many of its songs, that anger is implicit in the sound, pace, and performance of the music itself. And, more so than an American guitar band might, the band revels in the release of that anger in a way that is positive instead of dark. The late-teenaged Neds, writing from their West Midlands home, feeling trapped, are thus the same as Nirvana members writing in Aberdeen, Washington, Mark E. Smith writing in Manchester, the Wedding Present's David Gedge writing in Leeds. Boredom, anger, and the feeling that you're imprisoned by your life without knowing how to change it are not site-specific. I should note, however, that the town that Ned's Atomic Dustbin's members are from, Stourbridge, is also where the members of the Wonder Stuff and Pop Will Eat Itself are from. The "we've-got-to-move" pulse of all three bands is rooted in the depression of those surroundings. But, again, that depression is paralleled by similar conditions in towns like Aberdeen, Manchester, and Leeds. And, as I've suggested with Nirvana's "Smells Like Teen Spirit," the depression is not just expressed lyrically. There's a recognizable, almost tangible frustration that comes across musically, in each player's musicianship, in the strain of the vocals. It's about urgency, and that comes down to a lot more than words.

That frustration is also clear in the work of another band that I've lumped in with the grebos, the Wonder Stuff. Although some critics and fans would label the band as too poppy to be pure grebo, its music incorporates so many grebo characteristics that leaving it out of a discussion of the genre seems illogical. The band concentrates on a formula of revved-up power-pop mixed with biting, sharp lyrics, sung with venom by lead singer Miles Hunt. Basically, it's grebo pop. Attracting a fan base that is similar to that of other grebo bands—young, pissed off, schlepping unwashed from gig to gig, reveling in the volume and buoyancy of it all—the band has had huge success in England. There, its pop sensibility has allowed its fan base to expand beyond the initial grebo core to average record buyers, similar to the way Nirvana's "Smells Like Teen Spirit" appealed to more than just grunge fans. For the Stuffies (as they're called by fans) to cover the Jam's "That's Entertainment" single makes complete sense: Both bands superimpose spit-out vocals (which express pent-up anger more articulately than any lyrics could) and guitar grit over pop tunes. But, as with the effect of Jeff Koons's silver-coated blow-up bunnies, the Wonder Stuff mixes laughter with the spit. While the Jam was influenced by the politics and other dynamics of its Woking, England, surroundings, circa late seventies/early eighties, the Wonder Stuff is a product of its members' Stourbridge, West Midlands, late eighties/early nineties musical and cultural environs. In a grim, nowhere town, the Stuffies' response and escape is via snarling, revved-up bomp.

What makes the Stuffies particularly interesting is the dichotomy in their music between the cynicism of the lyrics and vocal delivery and the jubilance of the tempo, instrumentation, and musicianship. By sound alone, the Stuffies seem like a raggle-taggle party band. But once you catch the songs' bite, you're smirking through the smiles. Mere song titles express the band's "sell-me-another-bridge" conceit: "It's Yer Money I'm After, Baby" and "Give, Give, Give Me More, More, More" off 1988's debut LP, *The Eight Legged Groove Machine*; "Don't Let Me Down, Gently" and "Cartoon Boyfriend" from 1989's *HUP*; "Inertia" and "Welcome to the Cheap Seats" of *Never Loved Elvis* (1991). There's a distrust of society, a cynical suspicion of the world. Lyrics mention everyone from R.E.M.'s Michael Stipe ("Maybe") to Elvis Presley ("Mission Drive"), but these figures are included not for superficial name-dropping but because the references add specificity and evocative realism to lyrics that deal with real-life issues like parent/son shouting matches ("Mother and I"), feelings of confusion and inadequacy ("Maybe"), and infidelity ("Unfaithful"). But there's always a flippancy, a tongue-in-cheek optimism that comes from the juxtaposition of those lyrics with bubbly music as their soundtrack. The band's lead singer, Miles Hunt, has also become known, particularly during the band's first couple of years, for insulting his audience and other bands both on stage and in interviews. Certainly, there's a pomposity in that stance, but often his views speak for his audience's, and so they offer fans yet another way to connect to the band.

It's worth pointing out that the Stuffies rely heavily on frontman Hunt. Not only do the band members make a deliberate choice to offer him as the focal point of interviews and videos, but he also inevitably attracts the viewer's eye when the band is on stage. Certainly, the grebo movement is about a group mentality, like so many other alternative movements—and the feeling of community created by loads of teenaged fans, all dressed alike (and like their favorite bands), dancing together at a gig, is all-important. Some of the bands that best exemplify this ethic, like Mega City Four and Ned's Atomic Dustbin, are very much bands as opposed to a leader and his backing players. But there are just as many examples of grebo bands with dynamic frontmen, like the Wonder Stuff, Jesus Jones (fueled by leader Mike Edwards), and Pop Will Eat Itself (fronted by Clint Poppie). The explanation for this dichotomy comes down mostly to band personalities, as well as to the fact that no matter how much of a group ethic a band has, an aggressive, handsome lead singer is a potent asset. Certainly, there is always room for a charismatic leader in rock 'n' roll—and the fact that Hunt, underneath the shambles of tartan vest mixed with long hair, is handsome doesn't hurt either. Still, there's something "fuck-the-status-quo" refreshing about a band that is just a bunch of guys playing together, as is the case with a band like Ned's Atomic Dustbin. And, of course, the grime in grebo is part of its appeal. With its combination of joyful spirit and ramming guitars, it's as messy and fun a party as kids splattering themselves with finger paints. Both styles work: In an age of big-business rock 'n' roll and thought-about-every-little-point marketing, it's cool that bands can just settle into whatever mode is right for them. And for the grebo bands, as for British and American guitar bands, that mode is not across-the-board similar.

A band that is thoroughly the sum of its parts, without a standout frontman, is the Senseless Things. The members are marginally younger than those in Ned's Atomic Dustbin. They are newcomers to the scene. Unlike most of the grebo bands, they come from London (actually Twickenham, which is on its outskirts), and, again, some purists wouldn't label them as grebos because of that different geographic and cultural base. Yet musically, visually, and in the audience they attract, they're pure grebo. Combining a whiny high voice like that of the Neds, with a typical grebo out-of-breath tempo, guitar work reminiscent of a vintage American guitar band, the Replacements (the cover of whose 1984 *Let It Be* LP sits with the band on their inside sleeve cover), and almost tacky pop songs, I'd call their music bubble-grebo. Or, perhaps more appropriately, angry-young-man bubble-grebo.

While the Wonder Stuff's music is make-you-smile, the Senseless Things are downright goofy. Even the mere look of the cover of the band's debut album, *The First of Too Many* (on Epic Records), expresses that wacky side. It's a crazy, brightly colored, ornately drawn sleeve depicting a wild scene of strange creatures, a rocket ship and an airplane, a guitar made of a flower, and a smoking monkey. The graphic falls somewhere between a Ralph Bakshi cartoon, an underground comic, and a Woodstock poster. The songs themselves provide an inside look at modern life in realistic detail. For example, "Fishing at Tesco," a silly tale of buying dinner at the local supermarket, "Radio Spiteful" (which brings up issues like taking drugs and TV-news violence), and "Should I Feel It," about falling passionately in love with a TV junkie, all deal with the mundanities of real life. Sure, this subject matter could be called unsophisticated, but it's based in the real world in which kids grow up every day and written in their own language. Unfortunately, the band still doesn't seem classic-album-memorable, despite that mix of influences and true-to-life lyrics; but it does employ many grebo techniques, like mixing pounding guitars with reality, a touch of humor, and a heavy dose of charm.

Another London-based band that combines a mélange of musical influences, reality-based lyrics, and a sense of humor is the tongue-in-cheekly titled Carter the Unstoppable Sex Machine. The band is comprised of two normal South London lads who look more suited to a comedy routine than a pop band. One is skinny, the other huskier; they've dubbed themselves JimBob and Fruitbat. Hardly pinup stars, the pair are sort of a British version of Wayne and Garth from *Wayne's World* — except that they can actually write catchy songs and play instruments. The biting humor of their lyrics is in the tradition of the Monty Python/Goon Squad/Fawlty Towers school of comedy. Except that what this band is laughing at is pop culture. Its first album, spoofingly titled *101 Damnations*, features songs with titles like "The Taking of Peckham 123," "Good Grief Charlie Brown," "G.I. Blues," and "The Road to Demestos" – Demestos is a British household cleanser. The lyrics refer to shopping bags from England's Safeway chain, "OAPs" (old age pensioners), everyday London outskirts, including surrounding towns like Streatham and Peckham and Tulse Hill. Its second album, *30 Something* (the title an allusion to the television series), similarly includes pop references such as "Surfin' USM" (a twist on the Beach Boys' "Surfin' U.S.A."), "Say It with Flowers" (taken from an advertising slogan), and "Shoppers' Paradise." The songs refer to everything from Fairy brand dishwashing liquid to Southern Comfort to "the tubes of the Bec and Broadway" – the two subway stations in the London area of Tooting. In other words, JimBob and Fruitbat push aside the standard pop song locales like Hollywood and New York for very specific, deliberate personal references to the locations in which they live and the products they use. By so doing, the band merges, I suppose, pop music and pop culture. Clearly, these songwriters are children of the TV age and their lives are filled with an endless onslaught of pop culture. Time is spent eating convenience foods and riding the subway. Incorporating these activities into pop lyrics may sound banal – and perhaps that's the point. The message of the grebos, like that of the punks, is that to be average and normal is okay. Colloquial language and situations in the music of bands like Carter intensify the bond between band and listener by offering shared experiences. The combination of humor and the everyday makes the band's music like an episode of *Roseanne*: funny and cool and filled with a laugh-at-ourselves sense of community. And Carter's use of brand names matter-of-factly brings to mind, as the realistic setting of Sonic Youth's songs do, Warhol's Brillo pad boxes, Richard Prince's photographs featuring Marlboro cigarette imagery, and even Woody Allen's specific details of New York shops and locations in so many of his films, like *Annie Hall* and *Manhattan*.

But Carter goes further than just making superficial allusions to real life; the band takes clichéd phrases and twists them, leading its listeners to question the validity of their everyday assumptions. The song titles I listed above exemplify that twist, as do lines from songs off the first album: "Long distance information get me Jesus on the line" (from "Midnight on the Murder Mile"—based around the opening lines to Chuck Berry's "Memphis, Tennessee") or "life's just a bowl of cherries/for the fruit machine" (in "The Taking of Peckham 123"). Certainly, such lines are clever, amusing nods to musical and general clichés, but these augmentations of accepted phrases and sayings also represent a personalization by the band—an implication, as in the Clash's "I'm So Bored with the U.S.A." of the importance of speaking about what one knows directly to one's listeners instead of being infiltrated by someone else's culture. Like artistic expression as diverse as Italian neorealist cinema and the poetry of Robert Lowell, Carter's music is based firmly in the band's reality, which in this case is London—for better or for worse. On still another level, these lyrical twists parallel the bent details—too-loud guitars, fuzzed-out vocals—of alternative music.

Carter's music revolves around the same grebo grind as do the other bands in this chapter, although this band superimposes a clever use of samples (like another grebo band, Jesus Jones) and drum machines combined with guitars. That may sound high-tech, but with influences like the Clash and the Jam, the sound never feels as cold or sterile as the use of that technology might imply. The songs are basically pop tunes, as is clear on a track like "The Only Living Boy in New Cross" on the band's third album, *1992: The Love Album*. But what's captivating about the band is its sheer theatricality, which comes across both on record and live. Its music is as rooted in the English music hall tradition as in modern culture. Big and booming but always close to home, no matter how cynical or critical the song is (tracks like "Bloodsport for All," "Twenty Four Minutes from Tulse Hill," and "Midnight on the Murder Mile" deal with subjects like violence, murder, and drugs), you're still left smiling at the end. For kids brought up with scenes of war and gang violence on the news, these scenes are particularly resonant—even if they're laughing. Which, come to think of it, probably explains why the band's most devoted fans tend to be so young (under twenty). Kids can relate to the grebo-based energy of the sound, the lyrical references to their surroundings, the everyman-ness of the band members. Whether or not they take in the serious core of some of those lyrics, they've still had a great time.

Also from London is Jesus Jones, which, unlike most of the grebos, has a pivotal frontman, Mike Edwards, who writes and pro-

Mike Edwards of Jesus Jones

duces the band's material, plays lead guitar, and sings. The band also heavily uses samples. Nonetheless, like Carter, Jesus Jones still maintains a real sense of life both on record and particularly in the live show, which is based around musicians ripping away at their instruments, jumping around the stage. Musically, there are more dance elements in the band's work than in that of most grebo bands (with the notable exception of Pop Will Eat Itself). In fact, there are many critics and fans who would not call the band grebo at all. But since the core of Jesus Jones' audience, particularly in England, is grebo, I consider the band part of the genre. Certainly, in terms of the spirited, sample-friendly pound that is the band's sound, its real-life lyrics, and the look of both the band and its fans, Jesus Jones fits many grebo characteristics. Nevertheless, the band does have its own style. While grebos like the Neds and the Megas process their pop tunes through churning, overpaced guitars, Jesus Jones entangles its in almost techno-dance stuff—listen, for example, to "Move Mountains" (off the debut album, *Liquidizer*) and "Welcome Back, Victoria" (off the follow-up album). If the Megas are punk-inspired grebo, Jesus Jones is techno-dance, pop-inspired grebo. Certainly, the Jones' music is high-tech, but it's musically sophisticated enough to maintain a humanistic feel.

A key reason why Jesus Jones may not be labeled grebo anymore may well be their huge sales success, particularly in America, where "Right Here, Right Now," a single from the band's *Doubt* album, went to number one on the *Billboard* singles chart. The album went platinum. Unlike grebos such as Ned's Atomic Dustbin and the Wonder Stuff, who have had large alternative success in America but top ten status only in England, Jesus Jones diversified its fan base with its huge American commercial success, alienating some initial fans. Although the bulk of Nirvana's *"Bleach"*-era fans weren't alienated by the success of *Nevermind*, Jesus Jones has lost many of its early fans. It may be because Jesus Jones' "Right Here, Right Now" single seems lightweight in comparison to the grit of singles like "Move Mountains" and "Never Enough" off the band's earlier *Liquidizer* LP. The band's initial American fans may have also been put off by the heavy rotation of the "Right Here, Right Now" video—again and again, ages after college radio had been playing it, even though it's bland and predictable—on MTV.

Also dance-based within the genre is Pop Will Eat Itself, led by a charismatic if goofball frontman, Clint Poppie. From the West Midlands town of Stourbridge, like the Ned and the Stuffies, PWEI combines the churn of grebo with hard dance grooves, a sense of humor, and the cynicism and pop culture references of bands like the Wonder Stuff. In fact, one British single by PWEI is called "Touched by the Hand of Cicciolina," after the Italian porn film star/parliamentary official/wife of Jeff Koons. This hybrid is probably best epitomized by the single "Wise Up, Sucker," which is, on top of all those things, a dynamic pop tune. Most of the tracks on their RCA albums, *This Is the Day This Is the Hour This Is This!* (from 1989) and *Cure for Sanity* (from 1991), are more sample heavy and less well-structured-song than "Sucker." What's really notable about PWEI is its English fan base—very young (in the fourteen-to-seventeen range), dressed like the band members they love (with frazzled, mangled hair, grimy clothes, and eager grins), and willing to follow them from gig to gig. In other words, PWEI's fans personify the grebo aesthetic. They are die-hard allied to their band, and empowered by the sense of community they find at a gig.

There are other bands that were originally considered part of the grebo movement—namely Zodiac Mindwarp and Crazyhead—which are worth mentioning at least in passing. Neither band has the long-lasting musical quality of a band like the Neds, but both attract fans who wear similarly scruffy clothes and are attracted to a similarly accessible, revved-up sound. A more recent addition to the pack, the Levellers, mix grebo with celtic folk. Again, the band's songs don't have the indelible impact of other bands discussed in this chapter, but the band does have a knock-it-out live energy that is only hinted at on its studio albums, like 1992's *Levelling the Land*. The band's impassioned live shows have led some British fans, much like the Deadheads, to follow entire tours. Like the members of Carter and the Mega City Four, the band's young, predominantly male, baggy t-shirted fans buy their tour t-shirts and other merchandise with a zeal that produces a key source of band revenue.

Some people might include EMF in the grebo category. EMF is composed of a bunch of hovering-around-twenty kids who could easily be Jesus Jones clones. Like the latter, the band mixes dance beats and pop above the churn of grebo. I don't consider EMF part of the movement, however, because it has attracted a broader fan base than grebos have from the start with the international success of its single "Unbelievable." The one noteworthy quality about EMF— and I hope this doesn't sound too condescending—is that its members are extremely young. It's relevant that they, as well as the members of Ned's Atomic Dustbin and the Senseless Things, are the same age as their fans. That similarity offers another band/fan connection, and thus explains in part why fans are so moved by this music—it's as if the fans themselves are part of the bands, or at least in sync with them. Every song feels like an expression of themselves.

These young grebo bands exude a sense of fun and vitality. It's impossible to focus on grebo bands without going into their names and silly use of language. The grinding layers of guitar on a grebo record seem exuberant in comparison with, say, Hüsker Dü's dark sound, even when their lyrics are more cynical. That ebullience is reflected by their names—like Ned's Atomic Dustbin (taken from a *Goon Squad* sketch), the Senseless Things, Pop Will Eat Itself, and, of course, Carter the Unstoppable Sex Machine (just plain Carter or Carter U.S.M. to their fans). Those names seem almost disturbingly appropriate in their appeal to their audience because their young fan base is a generation of kids brought up on sit-coms and television cartoons. But to take things one step further, the theatricality and revved-up buoyance of these bands seems, to me, rooted in the English music hall and vaudevillian tradition. Whether they're the Neds or Jesus Jones jumping around the stage, the Wonder Stuff's Miles Hunt taunting his audience, or Carter backed by a flashy light show, the grebos are as much about spectacle—even if it's grassroots spectacle—as about extra-fast pacing or pretensionless grime.

That may explain why the coherent grebo fan base I've discussed exists primarily in England. Certainly, bands like the Wonder Stuff and the Neds have many American fans and have achieved loads of alternative/college radio success here. But America is so much bigger than England that most fans cannot follow their favorite band around the country the way they can in England. While British fans tend—as they have since punk—to be religiously into one genre of music and dress and therefore follow their bands around the country and even act like their favorite band members, American fans aren't so coherent. British fans have been since the late seventies/early eighties, as is shown by movements like the Mod Revival, Two-Tone, and New Romanticism. American fans think nothing of seeing the Neds one night and Social Distortion the next. A college radio station will sandwich a Mega City Four track between ones by, say, Sonic Youth and Curve, and by so doing offers its listeners a mélange rather than a genre. But the stuck-like-glue eagerness of grebo fans, and their youth, suggests that British young people are fed up with refinement and a stiff upper lip, fed up with being content with tradition and antiseptic cleanliness: These kids are bored and cynical but filled with energized potential. What the grebos offer—like Nirvana, like Sonic Youth, like Jesus and Mary Chain—is a release and expression of that energy.

The closest American parallel to both grebo fans and bands is probably the Red Hot Chili Peppers and their (huge) audience. The Chili Peppers, like another American band, Faith No More, pull together a mishmash of styles and influences – their music has elements of funk, soul, hardcore, and rap folded into its grind. It darts with the same hyperbolic energy as the music of a band like the Neds. The band members' clothes – like those of many of their devoted fans – are a decidedly postmodern, often humorous jumble of thrift shop, surfer, theater. More often than not, male fans expose bare, heavily tattooed, muscle-y California-brown chests. Of course, the Chili Peppers are now a huge band internationally. Their albums and singles have hit the top ten charts in many countries, like Nirvana's, and they've grown beyond the alternative realm. But, also like Nirvana, the band spent years playing small clubs, being played mainly on college stations, doing fanzine interviews, and working within other similarly alternative systems to come up through the ranks. What the Chili Peppers share most strongly with the grebos is a concentration on an intense, spastic, unquestionably pure live show without musical boundaries. In other words, the Chili Peppers defy the parameters of musical genres like funk, punk, soul, and rock and are more in-your-face than a race car going 120 miles per hour. Like a grebo band such as Mega City Four, the Chili Peppers pound across the stage, jumping and yelling, doing near acrobatics, performing shirtless. Next to a typical top-40 band, the Chili Peppers are like an old-fashioned European one-ring circus (which, frankly, is how their torpedo live show sometimes feels) instead of a glitzy, made-for-TV circus of the stars. While both are super-energized, one is more firmly based in reality.

To return to the British grebos, it's worth examining why women are, for the most part, excluded from the movement. That is not to say that there aren't female grebo fans – certainly, there are. But they're in the minority, and when they hang out with die-hard grebo fans, they tend to dress in the same baggy shorts or trousers, muddy Doc Martens or high tops, with dirty outgrown hair the same as their male counterparts, thus taking the spotlight off their gender. But this genre seems to be the only alternative genre with virtually no female band members. The only exception is in a band formed years after the mainstay grebo bands were formed: Back to the Planet, which features a female lead singer. Back to the Planet, however, is probably most accurately described as "dance-grebo." I find this phenomenon increasingly curious and, since these bands are so strongly connected to their fans, a little sad. If the grebos seem so keen to infuse their music with an effulgent energy that should appeal to a wide range of people, how is it possible that there are no women in any of the bands? It seems that, unlike female fans of American guitar bands or the miasmics, female grebo fans have no real role models. It's not fair to claim this is deliberate sexism—the irony of the situation is that one of the top engineer/producers on the grebo scene, who worked on Ned's Atomic Dustbin's *God Fodder*, Mega City Four's *Sebastopol Road*, and the Senseless Things' *The First of Too Many*, is a woman, Jessica Cocoran. Perhaps these bands formed as part of a "guy thing," like a basketball match after school or watching football on television on Sunday afternoon. Or, with a band such as Carter, it's like Monty Python: very funny, very British, and all male. Maybe it's just coincidence. It's just worth pointing out that, like an old-fashioned pub or a soccer match, grebo is both very British and predominantly male.

Yet it's the uniformity of the grebo fan base—young, male, pretention-free—which makes this music so compelling for its fans. The bond between performer and fan is strong and, come to think of it, rather poignant. Like punk, grebo is about empathy and connection between listener and performer. That connection is the same as the bond between a grunge band like Nirvana and its fans, and is, when it comes down to it, the bottom-line connection between the movements. But while grunge bands and fans seethe in shared aggressions, grebos revel in dealing with problems with laughter and wit. Nonetheless, both grebo and grunge bands speak to fans in a lyrical and musical language they can understand and use, and so both schools offer a remedy to the detachment of glitzy top-40 stars. Again, this attitude is the ethic of punk and, really, part of the alternative ethic as a whole. But while American grunge is about urban and suburban nowhere-to-run gloom, British grebo parties away its problems in the tradition of, as I've mentioned, the pub, the soccer match, or the music hall. Combined with nineties musical influences and an alternative ethic, that party has its own distinct sound and voice.

FEEDBACK
SIX
BANDS

For non–music heads, here's what feedback is: It's the squelchy, distorted sound of electric guitar signals being frazzled through amps, overloading those amps and electrical circuits to contort what would be clean guitar lines into something fuzzy but loud, unclear but intrusive—like a tornado of noise and music and edgy fury. It gets its name from the gory noise of electric guitar signals literally feeding back into amplifiers. Feedback is nothing new—it was an integral part of Jimi Hendrix's guitar style, the Velvet Underground's sound, early Who records. But alternative artists use feedback in a different way than those earlier artists did. And the use of feedback's moody fuzz in the alternative realm points to a cultural climate that is very different from that of the sixties.

By this point, it's probably obvious that I feel the use of feedback in alternative music metaphorically represents the confusing cacophony that is life in the late twentieth century. Sometimes, feedback is called "white noise" – like the noise of television static turned up all the way. And like that noise – like a pneumatic drill ripping apart the pavement – feedback is disorienting and hard to grasp on to. There's something intrusively disquieting about it. But it's also a sound that is just a given of urban life.

So far, I've delved into the way different bands assimilate "experiential churn" into their music – by blurring it out so that it's as if they're seeing life through dirty eyeglasses, by warping vocals so they sound "wrong," askew. Some of these bands, like Sonic Youth, My Bloody Valentine, Dinosaur Jr., and Nirvana, do integrate feedback guitar noise into their work. And some observers would simply lump the focal band of this chapter, the Jesus and Mary Chain, into that pile and say that the band simply represents the same confusion musically and culturally. To me, that's not giving this band the spotlight it deserves. It's a hugely important band, not in terms of musical sophistication, because that's simply not what it's about, but in terms of sheer musical impact. The band's first album, *Psychocandy*, along with the bulk of the rest of its work, is an exact expression of an alternative – and postmodern – mixture of traditionalism and deliberate negation or warping of that traditionalism. If any album musically actualizes the almost drugged-out confusion of life today, *Psychocandy* does. In addition, the band uses feedback in a way that is slightly different from the way miasma bands or American guitar bands do, and in different proportions. To understand its nuances is to understand how alternative bands use their own methods to twist musical norms.

When it was released in 1985, *Psychocandy* sounded so weird. If you didn't hear it then, it's hard to re-create that initial jolt. (Think of a 1990s teenager listening to the Beatles' *Sergeant Pepper's Lonely Hearts Club Band* for the first time and trying to imagine how groundbreaking it sounded in 1967, and you'll sense the same time lag.) Although clearly the amalgamation of a jumble of influences – from Phil Spector's girl groups to the Velvet Undergound – the Jesus and Mary Chain (or, more simply the Mary Chain, which is what some of its fans call the band for short) did something so new on that first album that it's still influencing bands today. Basically, the band used the feedback of their guitars as if it were an extra flute or violin or double bass. Given the space of an extra instrument, that feedback – otherwise known as distortion, something that is supposed to be twisted or strange—became an integral part of each song. While My Bloody Valentine blends vocals deep within each song's overall mix to take the spotlight off those "lead" vocals and equalize the vocals with the track's other instruments, the Mary Chain mixes its feedback loud and up, to show it off, to give the feedbacked sections the value of a solo by a choir's best singer or a band's virtuoso guitarist. Listening to songs like "Cut Dead" and "The Hardest Walk," you're left questioning just what is musicianship, what is beautiful, what deserves the spotlight and what doesn't.

One key quality of the band's music is that all that fucked-up feedback is piled on top of what otherwise would be classically structured, three-minute, stick-in-your-head pop tunes. In fact, on so many of *Psychocandy*'s tracks—"Never Understand," "Just Like Honey," "Inside Me"—you can't help thinking that if you stripped away all the steel wool squelch, you'd get what could be demos of some great lost pop band, circa 1962. And, frankly, when you see the Mary Chain's Reid brothers—with their shiny black leather, pimples, and mangled black hair—you can't help thinking that, like the Peanuts comic strip character Pigpen, underneath that grime they are just the boys next door.

It's important to draw the distinction between the fuzz of the miasmics and that of the Mary Chain. The miasmics use the whirr of feedback to replicate a fuzzy disorientation. Listening to their music, the listener feels lost and dazed; a My Bloody Valentine album sounds something like a more conventional rock album would if you listened to it whacked out on acid. The Mary Chain's brand of feedback, in contrast, sounds more like a chain saw gnarling its way through a tree. It's violent and dark; the experience is more like listening to a mainstream album with a migraine. If the Valentines are the fog of acid, the Mary Chain is the intensity and desperation of a throbbing wound or of just-been-dumped heartbreak.

It's also important to note that at the base of the Mary Chain's music is the grand melodrama of the Shangri-La's and the Ronettes and the cool pop of the early work by the Beach Boys. Like other alternative bands, the Jesus and Mary Chain takes traditional rock 'n' roll structures and limits and scrambles them. The classic, sing-along pop songs that lie beneath layers of feedback on Mary Chain tracks like "Just Like Honey," "Head On," and "Cool About You" regularly expose themselves like jelly gooshing after just the right bite of a greasy filled donut. It's that mix of sweetness and bite—beauty and

Jesus and Mary Chain: William and Jim Reid

the beast, if you will—that gives the Mary Chain's music such resonance.

The blend of old and new is, of course, a defining quality of postmodernism. By superimposing squelching feedback over a foundation of pop songs, the Mary Chain's music parallels the work of artists like Tim Rollins and the K.O.S. Rollins works with poor children from the South Bronx whom he's dubbed K.O.S. (Kids of Survival). The group takes yellowing pages from books by Gustave Flaubert and Nathaniel Hawthorne and uses them like a canvas, painting over them with their own artwork. Basically, they take classics and deface them, throttle them, mutate them to have some relevance in those kids' difficult world. In an analogous way, the Jesus and Mary Chain piles a cloud of feedback on top of girl-group-styled songs. The sound is sort of modern pop gore. But the feedback has an aural breadth akin to a trademark Phil Spector production. The majesty of that sound — also a key aspect of the Ramones' records, one of which, 1980's *End of the Century* LP, Spector actually produced — gives the Mary Chain's music an omnipresent nod to the vintage pop 45's. It also fills stage/ears/speakers with a can't-ignore-it command.

But the Jesus and Mary Chain uses more than layers of feedback to twist its almost bubble-gum structures. Lead singer Jim Reid's dry, un-focal-point, (once again) anti-singer's voice — sounding more like a kid singing along with a top-40 record in his bathroom mirror than a pop singer in a recording studio — adds a twist that you wouldn't find on a classic pop ditty. Lyrics like "You cut me dead/cut me down and kicked my head" and "Cherry takes me to the place above/with barbed wire kisses and her love" and "I want to die just like Jesus Christ" certainly aren't standard pop fare. But their songs *are* built around traditional verse-verse-chorus-verse-chorus-bridge-verse-chorus systems. They often feature pop sounds, like the "ba ba ba's" in "Cut Dead" or the classic fifties three-chord progression in "Kill Surf City," both of which could be straight out of the Beach Boys' catalog. Some songs feel more like strung-out cover versions than new compositions. "Sidewalking," which is thoroughly immersed in a T. Rex-ed sound, exemplifies that quality. Yet the combination of those true-to-influence devices underneath sheets of feedback, along with normal-guy vocals and lyrics that are at times drug-focused, sex-focused, macabre, or blasphemous, never feels traditional. It's the musical analog of, say, the Situationist artist Asger Jorn's "L'Avant-garde se rend pas": an old flea-market oil painting defaced with a drawn black mustache and goatee. It takes the past, waves hello at it, and then quickly, violently demolishes it.

The band's repeated references to the Beach Boys and California vintage sixties surf music run through its music like a Wagnerian leitmotif. On the *Barbed Wire Kisses* compilation of B-sides and demos, there is not only a demolished take of the Beach Boys' "Surfin'

USA" but also a dark, revved-up, surfer-on-smack song called, ominously, "Kill Surf City." Other songs, like "Never Understand" and "Inside Me," sound like Beach Boys songs being dragged through an oil slick. If postmodernism is about taking the past and negating it, then the Jesus and Mary Chain is decidedly postmodern; if alternative music is about subverting pop conventions so that they make sense to specific musicians as people and (ultimately) their contemporaries and fans, then the Mary Chain is unquestionably alternative. After all, you can't find two sets of more different brothers than the early-sixties Beach Boys' Wilson brothers—clean, sparkling, apple-pie white boys—and the Mary Chain's Reid brothers—spotty, dirty, topped with mushroom-cloud black hairdos, dressed in Velvets-era Lou Reed black leather and drainpipe trousers, speaking in heavy Scottish brogues. Southern California, they sure as hell ain't.

That unhyped, unmanufactured, real-life grit is, of course, the antithesis of a more image-conscious, mainstream star like, say, Madonna. The Mary Chain's message is that average kids from a bland little town (in their case, East Kilbride, near Glasgow in Scotland) can still synthesize their cool influences (albeit mostly American ones), add their own ideas to the pot, and—presto!—anyone can be a rock star. Of course, that democratic attitude is mirrored by many artists in other media—like, say, the Liverpool poets or Harold Pinter in his play "One for the Road." Like those writers, the Mary Chain never explicitly declares that "it's okay to be working class and from Great Britain." But by singing in their own accents and dealing with real-life situations in their lyrics, the band's members do offer an alternative to the "Americentrism" of, say, Madonna or Bruce Springsteen. Like the work of the Liverpool poets, the band's music is a real expression of its members' own experiences and lives. And understandably, it's easier for a working-class kid to empathize with the Mary Chain's attitude than with the sterile superficiality of most top-40 pop stars.

When the Mary Chain first began playing regularly in London and releasing its early British singles, like "Upside Down" (in late 1984), "You Trip Me Up" (in mid-1985), and, ultimately, its debut album, *Psychocandy*, which came out in England in late 1985 and early the next year in America, there were often complaints, confusion, and—sometimes—riots at their gigs. The band would play for twenty minutes, backs to the audiences, and then leave. The crowd noise at one of these incidents was captured – believe it or not – on a bootleg single called "There's a Riot Going On." And like a sixties happening, the Mary Chain warped its audiences' expectations of what they'd hear, of what a performance – and art – was. On record too, the band's music stretched a listener's definition of what music is. The intense, droning feedback on *Psychocandy* tracks like "In a Hole" and "Never Understand" sometimes sounds more like a churning drill than music. Like feedback in the music of the Valentines or Sonic Youth, juxtaposed with traditional melody lines, this music certainly makes the listener question traditional definitions of beauty and, I suppose, musicality. But the sound on *Psychocandy* – although in sync with the work of those other bands – is all its own. Like a spiky, unfinished hem on an expensive couture dress (a detail that can be seen on much of Rei Kawakubo's early-nineties Commes Des Garcons pieces), it's a modern merging of grit and beauty. And, like the music of My Bloody Valentine, the Mary Chain's sound gives the listener the sense that in the modern world of confusion and suffering, the only concept of beauty that is relevant must integrate the harsh with the ornamental. The mix evokes a homeless person sleeping outside a Chanel store or a Parisian motorcyclist zooming past the Arc de Triomphe on a superfast bike with his Walkman on – it's practically a survivalist tactic to blend tradition with elements of modern life. In today's world, for art to be meaningful as opposed to merely ornamental, it must incorporate some of the bite of the outside world.

All of which sounds quite cerebral – which, when the music was created in the mid-eighties, was hardly the intention. The Reid brothers were merely synthesizing their influences through a wall of noise. As is true with bands ranging from My Bloody Valentine to the Wedding Present to Dinosaur Jr., the barrage of volume offers a catharsis and a shared, like-it-or-not corporeality. Certainly, mashing that volume into a coffee-bean-grinder pile of white noise gives the Mary Chain a distinctive sound. Painfully clear examples of this recipe are *Psychocandy* tracks like "Taste the Floor," which turns the "middle eight instrumental section" of its standard pop song structure into the fuzzy growl of an electric can opener groaning around the lid of a can of peas. The frazzled beginning of "The Living End" equally illustrates this technique. This use of white noise also actualizes, as the miasmics do, the confusion of modern life: Their feedback is loud, disorienting, and sometimes hard to grasp. Tearing through sheets of feedback, the band offers the catharsis of a primal scream: The Reid brothers simultaneously actualize and release the rage and frustration of kids who are bored, dissatisfied, muddled, fucked up. The band's music offers the same release as that of Dinosaur Jr. or Nirvana but carries out that offer in a different way.

The Jesus and Mary Chain's mere use of feedback is in itself noteworthy, but what really matters is the fact that the band integrates that feedback into its music in hyperbolic proportions. The prevalence of feedback in the band's music has the boom of a symphony orchestra. Compare a more understated use of feedback—for example, in the Beatles' "I Feel Fine"—with the Mary Chain's gritty "Taste the Floor," and you'll hear the dark bite that heavy feedback adds.

Like many alternative bands, the Mary Chain takes listener expectations and twists them. Just as the miasmics take what could be the foundation for a classic song and wash it out, and a band like Dinosaur Jr. intensifies the same foundation with too-yelled vocals and spiky guitars, so the Mary Chain adds feedback—almost inserting it like cloves in an orange—to personalize their work, adding tension and grit. *Psychocandy* begins with the drumroll-please chopped mini-verses of an old pop song like the Crystals' "(Remember) Walking in the Sand" or the Shangri-La's "Leader of the Pack"—and then drops in machine-gun feedback like a terrorist hijacking a plane. Of course, that ripping apart of the status quo is in sync with punk, Dada, the Nouvelle Vague movement in French cinema, and the New German Cinema—with its motto "The old cinema is dead. We believe in the new one." But its pop-song base also gives the Mary Chain's music the same stick-in-your-head appeal as the jukebox hits it rips to shreds.

Postmodernism isn't 100 percent new or anarchic: Its referents are the forms and techniques of high modernism. Standard, traditional, oldies-station-structured pop songs provide a basic core for a variety of alternative sub-genres, but each band negates/changes/contorts elements of that core in its own musical way. Yet the Jesus and Mary Chain goes one step farther: Its music is a constant homage or, perhaps more correctly, a constant middle finger to the most classic of rock 'n' roll structures—the sweet pop ditty, as delivered by girl groups. While bands like Dinosaur Jr. and Nirvana launch off a general pop base—not rooting their song structures around one particular mainstream rock movement but several, negating conventional expectations that are the result of years and years of listening to loads of bands and styles — the Mary Chain's targets are clear: groups like the Shangri-La's and the Beach Boys. "Kill Surf City" indeed. It's almost as if the Jesus and Mary Chain's own compositions are actually throttled cover versions of existing pop songs. A song like "Just Like Honey" feels like a deliberate, pronounced, simultaneous homage to and defacement of classic pop in the same way that real covers like Dinosaur Jr.'s "Just Like Heaven" or the Afghan Whigs' "My World Is Empty Without You" do. Which is not to say that the Mary Chain or those other bands are dissing the earlier bands. It's just that, for alternative bands, the dissemination of girl-group pop songs necessarily includes fucked-up guitars and white noise feedback — in the tough-it-out world of today, mixed-in growl is the only way to handle the pop sweetness. For cynical kids raised on drugs and violence and the seven o'clock news, this alternative mixture of pop and noise is the musical version of eating a TV dinner on a recyclable tray: It puts pop conventions into a context that is relevant today.

Psychocandy exemplifies the band's feedback-pop style best. Spikier than anything they've done since, this growling and raw album from 1985 is glued to its influences but violently spitting at them as well. By the time the band recorded its follow-up, *Darklands*, in 1987, feedback was still an integral part of its sound but was given less of a spotlight in the mix. While *Psychocandy* tracks like "Sowing Seeds" and "The Living End" place feedback in the position of guitar solo or a star-quality vocal, on *Darklands* cuts like "Happy when It Rains" and the title track, feedback becomes just another part-of-the-band instrument. Which is not to say that the use of feedback is any less noteworthy on that second album. Integrating feedback deeper into each track's mix may seem to take away some of that feedback's shock value. However, at the same time, that *Darklands* formula is reminiscent of switching TV channels filled with infomercials and televangelists and homicide-a-day news, or running through a dial of mismatched radio stations too quickly. In other words, the combination actualizes the onslaught of too many impeti. For the Mary Chain, the way to update the standard pop composition of a song like "Darklands" or "Cool About You" — the way to give it some relevancy — is to add a layer of edgy feedback, even if it's not at the forefront as on *Psychocandy*. This impulse parallels Mark Morris's updating of *The Nutcracker* with hip costumes, battery-operated toys, and an on-stage television yule log in his 1992 adaptation, "The Hard Nut." Or, more simply, it's like a computer geek translating James Joyce's *Ulysses* into a code of machine-bites: a transliteration to speak to postmodern culture.

Along with the recurrent use of feedback, there is a recurring lyrical theme on *Darklands*—like a poet's repeated image throughout a volume of poetry. The titles—"Nine Million Rainy Days," "Happy when It Rains," "April Skies"—are the tip-off. Rain is a logical image: The fierce pound of a rainstorm is almost like nature's version of feedback. More important, the dank, dreary bleakness of a rainstorm parallels a darkness not only within the band's music but within the lives of many of its fans. If part of the appeal of bands like Nirvana and Sonic Youth is in the no-frills, depressed, "get-me-out" view of the world they often present, then that's some of the Mary Chain's appeal with these songs as well. So much of the imagery on the *Darklands* LP is almost suicidally desperate. Songs like "Darklands," "Fall," and "Nine Million Rainy Days" are first-person, intense accounts of life on the brink. And if you are fifteen, sixteen, seventeen, living in a "Plathian" world of feeling inadequate, those tales, like those presented in the lyrics of the Smiths, probably precisely articulate how you feel. So these rain-soaked lyric lines are as in tune with their fans' emotions as with the feedback that backs them.

Darklands was followed by the *Barbed Wire Kisses* LP, actually a compilation of B-sides, outtakes, and alternate versions of songs. In many ways, the album returns to the pinpointable musical targets of *Psychocandy*. This album includes "Kill Surf City" and the slaughtered cover of "Surfin' USA," which nukes the Beach Boys. The band not only covers—albeit hodgepodge sloppily—Bo Diddley's "Who Do You Love" but also includes a track tongue-in-cheekily titled "Bo Diddley Is Jesus." There is an element of the absurd—when you remember that the Reid brothers are two spotty kids from the town East Kilbride, Scotland—in these shooting-gallery tributes to pop music icons. Somehow—only vaguely, only now and again—these tracks feel like Jeff Koons's sculpture of a white Michael Jackson, like a strange mix of elements and cultural backgrounds and art that isn't 100 percent convincing. But those covers and pointed songs do highlight the mix of classic tunes and feedback layers which is the key to the band's sound.

The band's next two albums, *Automatic* (1989) and *Honey's Dead* (1992), are, for the most part, more direct: They tip just slightly closer to the mainstream. Nonetheless, the songs are still jolted by feedback, although that feedback is their driving force, as it is on *Psychocandy*. On *Automatic*, songs like "Here Comes Alice" and "Blues from a Gun" are more about their raunchy drive than a gory outburst of feedback clamor. Admittedly, *Honey's Dead* features tracks like "Reverence," which bites with an almost sleazy combination of feedback and the refrain "I want to die just like Jesus Christ," repeated over and over, like something between a pop chorus and a death knell. Yet tracks like "Far Gone and Out" and "Almost Gold" (which might as well be an echo-chambered, nineties cover of the Ronettes' "Baby I Love You") are just more straightforward than the band's early work. On these later albums, the band changed the proportions in feedback-to-song ratio. Once used in unavoidable overload, feedback is an accessorizing ornament on an LP like *Honey's Dead*.

By the time *Automatic* was released, the band had become very successful in alternative circles in America. With its pop-song base and post-*Psychocandy* clear production, even if it does include feedback, the Mary Chain, after a couple of years of only cult status in America, began to receive loads of airplay on alternative radio stations, and on MTV's alternative shows *Postmodern MTV*, *120 Minutes*, and *Alternative Nation*. While its initial formula of classic pop with feedback sounded so rebellious and angry, the Mary Chain's more recent work is just a touch safer and appeals to a broader base. Certainly, the band still belongs in the alternative realm and works within alternative systems. Nevertheless, these are larger alternative systems: The commercial alternative radio stations sell advertising time and broadcast the accessible end of a college radio station's roster. In a similar vein, in 1992, the band toured as part of Lollapolooza 2, a touring festival of alternative bands modeled after England's end-of-summer Reading Festival. But just as their music began to reach more people and lose some of its early angry-young-man venom, I began to find it less interesting.

Consistent, however, throughout the band's career has been the look of its album covers, which parallels its music perfectly. Both the music and the cover art are loud, blurry, with the frazzled energy of a kid whacked out on drugs. On the cover of *Psychocandy*, both Reid brothers are out of focus, secondary in importance to the hazy, patchy, white backdrop and black and red lettering. One brother is reclining, small and fuzzy; the other is shown larger, looking half-stoned and clearly disinterested. A lone drum hangs out in the photo as well, for no apparent reason or connection. *Darklands*, *Automatic*, and *Honey's Dead* all feature blurry color photographs: The front and back of *Darklands* feature an out-of-focus, washed-out color shot — presumably from a television set — of what looks like (who can tell? it's so fuzzed-out) the band, a fire, and a column of television sets. *Automatic*'s front cover is a foggy photo of the Reid brothers inside a star, on the back cover there is a blurry portrait of the still band with a moving camera. *Honey's Dead* features a ghostly, faded, beiged-out portrait of a girl's face, like a medieval tapestry wilting away. These covers offer the same metaphorical expression as the band's music. The colorful, captivating fuzz visually parallels the band's use of feedback. Both are confusing, hard to decipher, and add a frenzied energy to the mix; both metaphorically replicate the confusion of modern life. While the miasmics' covers are faded, overexposed, obtuse (as on My Bloody Valentine's *Isn't Anything*, Ride's *Nowhere*, Catherine Wheel's *Ferment*), the Mary Chain's are Polaroid colorful. The covers visualize the jolt of machine-gun feedback on songs like "Taste the Floor" and "The Living End," which musically transliterate the in-your-face confusion of fifty cable channels of commercials and dial-a-porn in the middle of the night, or the intrusion of a phone salesman calling blindly to solicit his wares.

The group's LP covers capture the mix of directness and fog that is the key to the Mary Chain's sound. Musically, the Mary Chain, whose sound is fuzzed with feedback but alludes constantly to classic pop and rock conventions, is somewhere between the miasmics and the American guitar bands. It's interesting to note that the one LP cover that isn't bright and graphic, *Honey's Dead*, was released when the miasmics were still trendy. And it makes sense that the album's 1992 release was preceded by a British tour featuring Dinosaur Jr. and My Bloody Valentine along with the Mary Chain.

If the Jesus and Mary Chain's disconcerting mix of pop tunes and growl, its use of feedback, and its covers haven't grabbed you, chances are the name has. While the miasmic bands often parallel their whishy music with amorphic names (Slowdive, Curve, Ride, and so on), and a name like "the Cocteau Twins" lodges you straight into that band's arty vision, the Mary Chain's name is about shock value. The "sacrilege" of juxtaposing straight-out-of-the-Shangri-La's-wall-of-sound pop writing like "Never Understand" with grimy feedback (talk about "barbed wire kisses . . .") is eye opening. It is equally blasphemous for these band members to rip "Surfin' USA" to shreds and perform twenty-minute sets with their backs to the audience. There's no heavy religious imagery at work in the band's music or image. The name is merely a parallel of Marcel Duchamp hanging a urinal on a museum wall or Madonna selling a book of sex photographs — shock for shock's sake.

The Mary Chain's pop-song-feedback formula has influenced a load of bands. And although I classify the miasmics as Velvet Underground–based feedback and American guitar bands as Stooges/Neil Young–based, *Psychocandy* is regularly cited by many guitar bands as, if not a direct influence, a record they admire. As I mentioned, in 1992 the Mary Chain toured England with Dinosaur Jr., My Bloody Valentine, and the lighter-weight Blur; in America the band was on the Lollapolooza package tour with Lush, Soundgarden, and Pearl Jam and on its own tour with Curve and Spiritualized. These bills seemed musically coherent, in part because each band's music shares tangential links, like feedback or super-loud guitar volume, with that of the others. Remnants of the band's exploding pop noise can be seen in the work of bands like the Telescopes (on European-only albums like 1989's *Taste*, on the small British indie label What Goes On, and *Trade Mark of Quality*, from 1990 on Fierce Records, neither of which was released in America), and Loop (on its 1990 Beggar's Banquet album, *A Gilded Eternity*). Spacemen 3, who eventually splintered into the bands Spiritualized and Spectrum, also echo with the Mary Chain's sound. Although these Chain disciples, like the band that influenced them, may not attract the coherent fan base — including dress and dance styles — that a band like Nirvana does, they do offer a specific and unique release of pent-up aggression and frustration.

Whereas My Bloody Valentine's influence on a bunch of bands — all of which seemed to reach the press/label/radio spotlight at around the same time — snowballed, the Mary Chain's impact has been more gradual and so somewhat subtler. Nonetheless — and this is why the group deserves a microscopic analysis in the context of this book — the Mary Chain does exemplify how alternative bands fit into the postmodern realm. The band refers to its rock 'n' roll heritage but also comments on and negates tradition by including lashings of feedback and real-life details. Although this is what other alternative bands do, listening to even one Jesus and Mary Chain track proves the band uses alternative devices in its own way.

The Jesus and Mary Chain is also, turned up loud, like a super-charged combination of an oldies station and frazzled static, but it's that firm grounding in the modern world that gives its music a feeling of, well, appropriateness. The Mary Chain has sounded right since *Psychocandy* came out in 1985, just as the Sex Pistols and the Clash sounded so right in late-seventies London and Nirvana sounds right in early-nineties America. It's a question of addressing — without words, as well as with them — people's concerns. And for masses of angry, pop-culture-bred kids, the Jesus and Mary Chain does just that.

ART SEVEN BANDS

So far, I've discussed movements and bands that express their alternative-ness through aggressive, your-parents-would-hate-it ways: growling guitars, volume-on-top-of-volume feedback, a stoned, dog-like anti-singer's voice. This chapter focuses on what I call "art bands"—groups who embody the alternative ethic not with gritty, spiky anger but by adding beautiful, romantic details—albeit in an alternative way—to pop structures. Art bands are sort of a rock 'n' roll transliteration of chintz wallpaper on a dirty urban apartment wall. Nonetheless, these bands subvert the structures and systems of the musical mainstream as much as a band like Nirvana does. It's just that their means is analogous to a painter like Joan Mitchell using classic oil paints and brush strokes in a climate of postmodern Julian Schnabel smashed plates and horns splattered with shit-colored paint on an abused canvas. Simply put, art bands are about beauty more than bite.

By twisting pop structures with airy angelic vocals – as is the mode d'emploi for the band at the center of this genre, the Cocteau Twins – art bands are just as subversive of listener expectations as feedback-laden bands like the Jesus and Mary Chain and grunge meisters like Nirvana and Sonic Youth. They just do it in a gentler way. Covering their single and album sleeves in beautiful, artistic, anti-traditional-rock 'n' roll artwork, layering their music with musical details that are disarmingly lovely instead of gnarled out, art bands reject the mainstream with grace rather than aggression. Thus, they too offer an alternative. If anything, a band like the Cocteau Twins proves the breadth of the alternative realm. Although I find the term "alternative" useful because it defines what, for me, basically amounts to musical postmodernism, juxtaposing art bands with the brasher bands I've discussed proves that the term "alternative" refers to a wide array of musical styles. Although this chapter will examine the parallels between the Cocteaus and the louder bands, their musical means is markedly different, as is clear from their first few notes.

The band's name is the first tip-off that it presents a handful of ironies along with its music: The Cocteau Twins are, in actuality, a band of three. Their name is a nod to poet/artist/filmmaker Jean Cocteau; it represents an antithesis to the humble origins (in Grangemouth, Scotland) of the two main creative forces in the band, namely, Elizabeth Fraser, a built-like-a-bird lead singer with the voice of ten angels, and Robin Guthrie, who is big and burly, and responsible for much of the band's production and overall sound. Although these contrasts are noteworthy, the most substantial dichotomies at work are musical ones: the clash of shimmery guitars with an electro-drum machine; the confusion of songs with pre-Raphaelite titles and unintelligible lyrics; the surprise juxtaposition of electric guitars against Fraser's exquisite voice.

That voice – God! What a voice! – is a logical place to begin decoding the band. Sometimes it's almost operatic (on *Victorialand* tracks like "Fluffy Tufts" and "Throughout the Dark Months of April and May"). Sometimes it soars and peaks like a seagull flying over a body of water, as you can hear on *Treasure*'s "Lorelei" and songs like "Head over Heels" and "Sugar Hiccup." Alternately it squawks, almost too sensuously, like the Bulgarian Women's Choir (on *Heaven or Las Vegas*'s "I Wear Your Ring") and floats like the most buoyant dream soundtrack to a diaper commercial, which is

The Cocteau Twins

evident on the same album's "Fotzepolitic," on *Blue Bell Knoll*'s "Carolyn's Fingers" and "Athol-Brose," on the gorgeous "Pearly Dewdrops Drop" and countless other Cocteau tracks. That voice seems to have a life and energy of its own. Like a poem by Arthur Rimbaud, Fraser's vocals are nonstop jubilant, even – as paradoxical as it may sound – when the mood is dark. They soar like the pouch of wind underneath a bird's wing. As the antithesis of most of the real-people vocalists I've examined so far (think of the contradiction in terms of a duet between Fraser and Nirvana's Kurt Cobain, or the Fall's Mark E. Smith), her voice is just plain beautiful.

While other alternative bands – most notably the British and American school of guitar bands – revel in their average-ness, Fraser's voice is unattainable, distant. On songs like "Cherry-coloured funk" and "Carolyn's Fingers," her vocals are layered on top of each other like a choir of angels. There's something as British as tea and scones, as old-fashioned as an antique tapestry about those vocals – they sound vaguely medieval, vaguely church-like, some-what foreign. But what makes those vocals fit into the alternative realm – and, I suppose, into the scope of this book – is that they are folded into sheets of electric guitar. As Nirvana and Sonic Youth twist their rock 'n' roll base with guitars tuned up too loud, too fast, too enraged, the Cocteaus throw listeners for a loop with Fraser's voice. If Kurt Cobain's voice is anti–mainstream rock 'n' roll, Fraser's is anti–rock 'n' roll period. While the ferocity of Cobain's voice can be equated with the roar of an electric guitar, Fraser's seems to pull those guitars into an almost classical vein. As Nirvana is shards of a broken beer bottle smashed in a brawl, the Cocteaus are a stained-glass church window. But although Fraser's voice sounds so different from Cobain's, hers is as cathartic and refreshing next to the blandness of top-40 as his is. While his scream is the battle cry, Fraser's soothes the savage beast.

Many art bands feature voices along the same angelic lines. For example, Dead Can Dance mixes crystalline female vocals above its synth-meets-medieval-revels sound on albums like 1988's *The Serpent's Egg* and 1990's *Aion*. Lush, a band that blends somewhat Cocteauish vocals with jarring guitars, released several pre-LP EPs produced by Cocteau Twin Robin Guthrie and is often compared to the Cocteaus. It makes sense that both those bands are signed, at least in England, to an independent label called 4AD, the Cocteaus' original base. It is logical that 4AD also released two albums of traditional Bulgarian choric singing under the titles *Le Mystere des Voix Bulgares, Volumes One* and *Two*. And the band that many critics describe as an amalgamation of the Cocteau Twins and the Smiths, the Sundays – featuring the lead vocals of Harriet Wheeler, who sounds like a little-girl-lost version of the Cocteaus' Fraser – is often described by the head of 4AD, Ivo Watts-Russell, as one of the bands he wishes he'd worked with.

In a standard pop song – from one by Diana Ross and the Supremes to one by Madonna – vocals are spotlighted on top of other instruments to express lyrics and act as the record's focal point. With the Cocteaus, Fraser's vocals are pedestaled ten times over. They are simply the center of attention. With a band like Nirvana, songs are built on a pop base and stray from there. Certainly, one of the personalized elements that can slide the songs into the alternative realm is a too intense, too real, too gritty voice like Kurt Cobain's, as Nirvana songs like "About a Girl," "Polly," and "Lithium" prove. With the Cocteau Twins, that base is merely alluded to, but not exactly used. Tracks like "Iceblink Luck," "Carolyn's Fingers," and "Pearly Dewdrops Drop" have their moments of near-verse-and-choruses, their catchy lines, but they don't start rooted in a pop tradition like songs by Nirvana or the Jesus and Mary Chain do. It feels as though the band's music is as based in jazz improvisation or classical music as in rock 'n' roll. And Fraser's voice is so much a centerpiece that the songwriting, no matter how strong the guitar lines are, must revolve around her. Which is not to say that the Cocteaus don't refer to previous rock 'n' roll structures, because they do. But their music does work at a further distance from those classic structures than that of many of the other bands discussed in this book. Like a Martha Stewart makeover on a plain white room, the Cocteaus add so many personal, ornate details that it's hard to find the shell they started with.

In previous chapters I've mentioned the lyrics of the Clash, Nirvana, Dinosaur Jr., and the exorcised-ness of their delivery. With directed, emoted vocals, their literal meaning is almost redundant. The listener understands the basic rage, anger, and target of their vocalists without even needing lyrics. And, as I've also pointed out, in songs like Nirvana's "Smells Like Teen Spirit" and virtually everything by the Fall, even if you wanted to know what the lyrics were going on about, you couldn't. They're nearly unintelligible. This cryptic wordplay is omnipresent in the Cocteau Twins' music, too; however, with a band like the Fall, you get the feeling that an intelligent—hey, at least a coherent—lyric exists. With the Cocteau Twins, even when you can make out snippets of words, it sounds as though Fraser is singing in a weird mix of a lost Arabic language and baby talk. On tracks like "Oomingmak," "Aloysius," "A Kissed Out Red Floatboat," and "Millimillenary"—on virtually all the band's recorded output—that angel's voice runs through what seems like a barrage of meaningless sound patterns. Even on the 1990 album *Heaven or Las Vegas*, when critics reveled in their ability to almost understand the band's lyrics, the operative word was still "almost." On songs like "Fifty-fifty clown" and "I wear your ring," you can just about hear a few English words in a row. They just make no sense in that row, like some weird haiku in a strange exotic language that sounds great but means absolutely nothing to the reader. Those literally anti-meaningful lyrics make the music no less beautiful. They add an off-kilter twist—not unlike Sonic Youth's open-tuned guitars—to what the Cocteaus do.

And, if Sonic Youth's guitars actualize—if only musically—the off-kilter, sometimes surreality of modern life, then so do vocals that are beautiful but unintelligible, and so unattainable. It's like watching a cable porn show in the middle of the night—those lyrics are something you can witness but never really become a part of, approach but never quite reach. Taking the focus off lyrics forces listeners to experience the music on a more abstract level—to concentrate on the emotions and expressions within the music as music instead of on the lyrical content. Of course, the Cocteaus encourage similar feelings through a variety of other devices with their music as well—for instance, by changing accepted, top-40 ratios of guitar to vocals, extending and turning up periods of feedback, and fuzzing guitar solos into a haze.

It could be said that deconstructing lyrics into nonlyrics is a major heavy-duty theoretical gesture, and I suppose in some people's eyes it is. But I don't think it's as academic as all that. For me, the Cocteaus share the same energized cry as Nirvana and Sonic Youth and My Bloody Valentine, even though they express it differently musically. The band expresses, albeit gently, a dissatisfaction with the musical norm, with the sweet, clean, oh-so-perfect world of mainstream pop. For those other alternative subgenres, like miasma bands and American guitar bands, dismissing the musical status quo means bludgeoning it through volume and noise. For the Cocteau Twins, it means replacing elements that don't work (like easily pinpointable lyrics) with ones that do (like Fraser's amorphic vocal style). If the purpose of a vocalist on a traditional pop record is to transmit lyrics and their meanings to the listener, the combination of Fraser's voice and the band's nonlyrics completely inverts that purpose. On the Cocteau Twins' records, Fraser's voice is an added instrument and is there to add another beautiful layer to the band's music, not to impart any stories or meaning per se. Sure, a vocalist like Nirvana's Kurt Cobain gets across some of the ethic of his lyrics through mere guttural vocal style, but his lyrics are, at least in quick spurts, possible to understand, unlike Fraser's, which are a constant blur. And, as a guitar or drum solo, her voice sometimes seems to have a life of its own, which helps give the music direction (or seeming lack of it) and drive.

But the inchoate quality of the band's music doesn't stop with Fraser's lyrics: The song titles are equally cryptic: "Frou frou foxes in midsummer fire," "Fotzepolitic," "The Itchy Glowbo blow," "Ella megalast burls forever"—to pull just a few of the more goofy-sounding ones as examples. Precisely what any of these titles mean is anyone's guess. For that matter, who knows what these songs' lyrics are, let alone what they mean. If an alternative band like the Smiths or the Fall puts more-than-substantial pop lyrics under an enlarger, the Cocteaus do the inverse. The band blurs its lyrics like a watercolor painting so they are unintelligible. It could be said that this lyrical haze parallels the musical one the miasma bands employ to express the confusion of today's world. In the land of the Cocteaus, gibberish means as much as a meaty sentence.

Certainly, many alternative bands use somewhat cryptic song titles. This technique is best exemplified by the miasmics, like Ride and Chapterhouse, who use song titles like "Pearl," "Vapour Trail," and "Taste" to suggest an overall mood instead of a specific plotline. Nirvana titles, like "Sifting" and "Blew," certainly fit this bill as well. But none of these titles are weird like the Cocteaus' are. Through their bizarre song titles, the Cocteaus express their refusal to conform to ordinary pop music boundaries, let alone to the confines of the English language. The boom of Fraser's voice suggests a bursting out, beyond borders—one of which, it seems, is meaningful language. And there is the implication that if the band wants to have nonsensical titles and nonlyrics and an effulgent lead vocalist, then that's their prerogative. It's sort of the musical equivalent of the any-hemline-will-do women's fashion attitude of the nineties versus the couture dictated styles of the fifties. And if alternative music is about twisting listener expectations, these titles sure as hell fit the bill.

But the Cocteau Twins' music is not just a lush, arty frolic through a beautiful—if obscure—musical garden. There's more at work than just Fraser's jewelly vocals and that use of weird, nonsensical language/nonlanguage. Those vocals are backed with shimmery, but unquestionably electric, layers of guitar—whooshing steadily along (on songs like "Pearly Dewdrops Drop," "Pitch The Baby," "Spooning good singing gum"—hell, on just about every track), piled one on top of each other like bodies crammed into a fifties American telephone booth. In a way, it's a wall of guitar sound—softened, soothed, like a freshly bathed child tucked in a blanket or drinking hot chocolate from a Beatrix Potter mug. But although those guitars don't assault your ears the way that, say, Sonic Youth's do, they're an equally vivid alternative statement: If the rock and pop mainstream pulls guitar lines along a contained, directed track, the Cocteaus' whirling, almost ambient guitars are as much a twist of accepted norms as Sonic Youth's sometimes atonal-sounding guitar bursts are.

In a sense, the band's meandering guitar work parallels Fraser's voice: beautiful, sometimes nearly classical sounding, blustering along on its own momentum. If a traditional pop song is fueled by the tightly mapped-out bars of its songwriting, then the Cocteaus' vocals and guitars have a life of their own – blown around like a kite on a windy day. Of course, the band is not improvisational – its songs are properly written and structured. Its structures aren't conventional ones, just as Sonic Youth's tunings aren't conventional and the Jesus and Mary Chain's proportion of feedback isn't conventional. While a band like Jesus and Mary Chain or Nirvana starts with a pop-song base and subverts it, the Cocteaus refer just enough to that base to acknowledge it and then stray off into their own territory. If Nirvana's music is off-rock 'n' roll, the Cocteaus' is off-off-rock 'n' roll. The band's songs feel like a jazz improvisation, or, to use a nonmusical analogy, a chiffon scarf loosely, elegantly blowing in the wind, constantly being retied to focus the effervescent flow.

There is one big contrast in the Cocteau Twins' recipe: the drum machine. Throughout the band's work, which is so passionate and vibrant, there are synthesized drumbeats instead of a live drummer. This device adds a constant feeling of cold, man-made sterility in sharp conflict with the other instruments – including Fraser's voice. On the band's early work, like "Wax and Wane" and "The Hollow Men" off 1982's *Garlands* LP, that drum machine gives the music an excessive melodrama and dates it alongside gloomy period pieces by, say, Japan or Siouxsie and the Banshees. As the band began to come into its own – on the 1983 *Head over Heels* EP and the 1984 *Treasure* album – those drums began to sound oddly stale. Underneath the over-the-top vitality of Fraser's voice, alongside Guthrie and third member Simon Raymonde's whirring guitars, the mechanized splat of the drum machine sounds gothic and flat. And on the band's most recent albums, *Blue Bell Knoll* and *Heaven or Las Vegas*, the drums sound as if they're remnants of some demo take that someone forgot to redo with a live drummer. Simply put, alongside the rest of the band, that drum machine is a contradiction in terms.

And maybe, when you pull away for a second, that's the point: The focus of the Cocteaus' music is so much on voice and guitar, blown along simultaneously but not exactly in unison, that perhaps the band feels that live drums would almost be too much, too intense. Admittedly, the pound of a drummer like Nirvana's Dave Grohl is almost exhausting combined with all that band's other equally forceful components. The fact is, however, that human drums would probably add the same lovely, textured nuances that Fraser's voice does. Nonetheless, the Cocteaus' blend of the hyper-humanity of Fraser's voice with the mechanics of the drum machine addresses a similar dichotomy in other media of postmodern art. For example, to return to some postmodern examples, Jeff Koons's tacky, giant reproductions of Hummel figures made by artisans in the finest Italian porcelain or Cindy Sherman's photographs of herself in clear, clear color, dressed in medieval costume in a faux-painting pose similarly merge art and high-tech mechanics. These pieces of art draw attention to the ability to maneuver and manufacture art in today's world. They acknowledge past setups (live drummers, Hummel figures, old oil paintings) and update them. They blend high art (the standard rock 'n' roll formula of guitars, bass, drum, vocals; handmade porcelain, museum-bound painting) and low art (drum machine, Hummel, bright color photography) into a heady stew. And so the Cocteau Twins' drum machine is one of the elements in the band's music which mark it as postmodern.

If other alternative bands are working against the musical establishment, the Cocteau Twins work against both the mainstream musical establishment and, in a sense, the alternative one as well. Unquestionably, they operate within alternative systems like college radio, fanzines, and clubs, but in each they're the exception to the rule. The Cocteau Twins, and the art bands they've influenced, are not overly loud or spiky or dangerous. They sound awfully, well, alternative next to Sonic Youth or Ned's Atomic Dustbin or Jesus and Mary Chain. The band is sort of post-alternative: Its music acts as a postmodern text but doesn't fit precisely next to that of its contemporaries. And so the juxtaposition of the Cocteaus' music with that of other alternative artists is analogous, to pull a fashion-world example, to putting early designs by Christian Francis Roth — beautifully constructed, hand-sewn garments with felt cutouts of a crayon or candy attached — side by side with a dark, deconstructed piece by Commes des Garcons: Both comment on the past, both mix high fashion and low fashion, but one does it violently and one does it with gorgeous details and a smile.

Using visual analogies makes sense in describing the Cocteau Twins' music. The band's album and single covers, the bulk of which were designed by Vaughan Oliver and his design team, called first 23 Envelope and then v23, are intricate, obtuse, and sometimes bizarre. They ignore the usual commodity issues of album cover art (essentially, that the album sleeve is a music wrapper, like a chewing gum wrapper or a label on a can of beans, advertising what's inside), acting as more than mere container. These covers are just plain beautiful, from the lace-draped, somber cover of *Treasure* to the amorphic, pale pinky white with sundown-orange-outburst cover of *Head over Heels*. They parallel the band's music: gorgeous, with something oddly classical going on in a modern realm. The images are impossible to decode as a whole but offer quick tastes of intelligible meaning. These loose, lovely designs are so appropriate to the band's music that they have become integrally linked to it. When different designers put together the *Blue Bell Knoll* and *Heaven or Las Vegas* sleeves, they used many of Oliver's trademark languid techniques.

While many modern albums concentrate on just a front cover, Oliver's designs for the Cocteaus include lavishly designed booklets, gatefolds, inner sleeves, and actual on-disc and on-vinyl designed labels. The ornate covers of 4AD albums like *Aion* by Dead Can Dance are the first tip-off as to the type of music they contain. Oliver's work really is art and has been shown in galleries, which, of course, supports the theses of John Berger in *Ways of Seeing*, Robert Venturi in *Learning from Las Vegas*, and Fredric Jameson in "Post-modernism and Consumer Society," which is that in today's world the distinction between commercial, utilitarian graphic and museum-quality art is fuzzy—that album covers can hang in museums, that advertisements and neon signs and other accoutrements (hey! even pop songs) of modern life have artistic value.

But other bands, both alternative and non-alternative, have included art on their covers; the significance of cover art for the Cocteaus goes still deeper. Since the late eighties, much of the music business has been wrapped up in the debate over the use of sampling, which as I've said is the electronic borrowing of sonic details from previously recorded material integrated into new songs by other artists. Sampling hasn't been a focus of this book, since it is more prevalent in the dance music world. Most of the bands I've focused on are about live, no-bullshit guitar music. Some of them, like Jesus Jones and Ned's Atomic Dustbin, use samples in an integrated way, as if those samples are another instrument, unlike the based-on-the-sampled-song songwriting of an M. C. Hammer or Vanilla Ice. The point of the sampling issue in the midst of this album-cover-art discussion is as follows: It's not just that the Cocteaus' albums have beautiful covers, it's that they're new art, created expressly for their releases. Yes, the Cocteaus' art-heavy covers make a conscious commercial choice to refrain from direct commerciality. But they also make an effort to be new art, created for a specific purpose. Here's what I mean: While artists like Sonic Youth and Galaxie 500 use art on their LP covers, as is shown by the Gerhard Richter picture on *Daydream Nation*'s cover and the Eugene Atget photograph on the cover of *Today*, the Cocteaus' covers feature art made and photographed expressly for those sleeves. The care and in-sync design behind the Cocteaus' covers redefines those covers as an integral part of the music. For a band like the Cocteaus, the cover is as much an expression of the album as its vocals or (non)lyrics are. Shit, those album covers are a lot more congruent with the Cocteaus' music than the band's drum machines are, for that matter. Other art bands' album covers—like the Sundays' *Blind* LP and Mazzy Star's *She Hangs Brightly*, neither of which Oliver designed—have a look that is equally in tune with their music. The bottom line is that for art bands, cover art is not a mere afterthought or sales tool but a vital part of the overall musical package.

Oliver's covers are one of the trademarks of the 4AD record label, which was the Cocteau Twins' worldwide base up until the *Heaven or Las Vegas* album (although that album and its predecessor came out in America via a licensing deal with Capitol). Founded in London in 1980, 4AD is virtually the Motown of art bands. With a roster featuring the Throwing Muses, the Pixies (both of which were released in America via licensing deals), Dead Can Dance, This Mortal Coil, and later signings like Swallow, Pale Saints, and Red House Painters, the label has a coherent musical identity, with a reputation for lavish, collectible-looking record sleeves and packaging. There's something almost subversive about the label's aesthetic: It is a refreshing antithesis to a major label's focus on bottom-line cost effectiveness. With 4AD, silver ink and thick CD booklets, arty, inherently uncommercial, bands, and special collectors' ten inches are the norm. Fortunately, the huge European success of 4AD bands like the Cocteaus and the Pixies has given the label the cash flow to make this lavish packaging a reality. If the booming seven-inch vinyl single market amongst alternative consumers is an anti-mainstream statement in a world of CD's, then 4AD's concentration on packages that look more like gallery catalogs than record sleeves—and the Cocteau Twins' music in a climate of Madonnas and Whitney Houstons—makes the same statement.

For years, 4AD stayed away from an American label licensing deal. (This is where an American major label would release all the label's artists.) Instead, British 4AD signings inked American licensing deals on an artist-by-artist, and sometimes release-by-release, basis. Some releases, like Dead Can Dance's *Aion* and the wonderful first Pale Saints album, *The Comforts of Madness*, were available as imports only. In 1991, the label finally signed an American label licensing deal with Warner/Reprise and so combined for themselves the best of both major and indie worlds: effective distribution via WEA (which stands for Warner/Elektra/Asylum) with the artist concentration of an indie. In a sense, that deal—like a similar one set up between British indie Mute and Elektra in 1990—is the analog of major labels aggressively signing bands like Nirvana, which got their start on indie labels, working within the indie systems. The success of bands like R.E.M. and the Cure, first within alternative systems and then beyond them—not to mention the way the scope and influence of those systems has expanded—has made major labels respect their viability. So entire label licensing deals, maintaining the indie's identity, are now signed.

Some time after 4AD signed its U.S. deal, it reissued a lavish boxed set of albums by the unusual band This Mortal Coil, a band very much in sync with the Cocteau Twins. What makes the band unusual is that its amorphic bunch of musicians is focused around— as strange as it may read—4AD's president, Ivo Watts-Russell. "Focused" is the key word in the band's set: more than performing himself, Watts-Russell brings together different musicians and tracks as the project's music ringleader. All three This Mortal Coil albums— 1984's *It'll End in Tears*, 1986's *Filigree and Shadow*, and 1991's *Blood*— feature a jumble of guest vocalists and musicians. The songs include the Cocteaus' Elisabeth Fraser doing a glorified take on Tim Buckley's "Song to the Siren," as well as other covers performed by the members of alternative bands like the Pixies, Throwing Muses, and Shelleyan Orphan. Although a great deal of the "band's" music is an almost ambient brand of dramatic synthesized instrumentals, each album's highlight is its arty clutter of cover versions of songs by the likes of Tim Buckley, Big Star and their drummer Chris Bell, the Talking Heads, and Wire. Maybe it seems self-indulgent for the label's president to be releasing his own records, but think about the creativity that shows in comparison to the three-piece-suited, older heads of major labels. As an artist himself, Watts-Russell can empathize with the needs and concerns of his artists. It would be hard to imagine the president of a major label putting out his own records. And 4AD is not the only label with a sometime-artist head: Mute's Daniel Miller released records under the name the Silicon Teens, and Creation's Alan McGee has released several albums by a band he's in, Bif Bang Pow. Washington, D.C.–based labels Dischord, TeenBeat, and Simple Machines are all run by the lead singers of the main bands on their labels (Ian MacKaye of Fugazi, Mark Robinson of Unrest, and Jenny Toomey of Tsunami, respectively). Just as alternative music rejects top-40 radio, it rejects the notion that a record label president must be a desk-jobbed businessman. If anything, label presidents who have their own bands prove to the artists on their roster that the priority is music over profit.

Unlike so much alternative music, Watts-Russell's This Mortal Coil is based around a recording studio instead of a stage. The band is like the Cocteau Twins in this respect. Although the Cocteaus do play live, they differ from most alternative bands in the live arena. All the other bands I've addressed in this book are live players. The gig is the place where their booming energy comes across most vividly, where fans can hang out with like-minded/like-dressed/like-dancing fans, where the in-your-face reality of the band members, both as musicians and people, literally comes to life. While the Cocteau Twins do play live and tour, their live show doesn't have the same assertive, dramatic punch as shows by, say, Dinosaur Jr. or My Bloody Valentine. Certainly, Fraser going through the vocal contortions of her singing style is great to hear live, but the rest of the band flanks her, standing near-still. Sure, they sound fine, but they look as though they're merely running through the motions. The Cocteaus' live show (which, compared to the live shows by the other bands, might be better called an anti-show, since there's no spectacle) lacks the tornedo force of shows by bands like Sonic Youth and the Jesus and Mary Chain. And maybe that's the point: Whereas those bands' music knocks you over the head, the Cocteaus' floats over you like a cloud. The same could be said of the live shows of other art bands like Dead Can Dance and the Sundays, who tightly rehearse for gigs that are more precise and less invasive than those of most alternative bands. The right thing to do at a Dinosaur Jr. gig is to put on your Doc Marten boots and mosh-dance in a sweaty crowd; the Cocteaus' music, even live, is best heard sitting down. A chiffon skirt or pale-pink lipstick would probably make the most fashion sense. If a band like Dinosaur Jr. is a shot of Jack Daniel's, the Cocteau Twins are a Victorian cup of herbal tea.

If you went to a Cocteau gig, you'd probably notice a much less coherent fan-base than at a Dinosaur Jr. or Sonic Youth show. The loud, rip-it-out-of-you guitars of so many of the bands discussed in this book are the ultimate catharsis for a specific type of fan: young, often male, using music as one method to deal with confusion, despair, loneliness, unemployment, boredom, whatever. And as I've said before, fans of American guitar bands have been labeled "slackers." The other band genres I've discussed so far — British guitar bands, grebo bands, feedback bands — all attract their own fans. The point is that each fan group's mode of dress and behavior is specific. And each band's members usually come from the same social demographic as their fans do and dress and act in a similar fashion. Fans get that natural, instinctive sense that they belong, and in this respect, music is their drug or religion or a diary filled with scrawled secrets. Art bands, in contrast, offer a cathartic space that provides a refuge in which fans can deal with and release the same problems and release shared frustrations and anxieties. It's more of an interior process than an exterior release. But for the Cocteaus and other art bands, the fan base is composed of a much broader demographic than exists for the other bands. Cocteau fans dress lots of ways and are all different ages. The band's music is cleansing in the way a beautiful Monet painting is cleansing, but it's sure as hell not the soundtrack to which you'd get your aggressions out.

While the Cocteau Twins have certainly influenced specific bands, like the Sundays and a younger Irish band called the Cranberries, its impact is more complex than that. The Cocteaus prove that to be alternative you don't have to make the loud, growling sounds that other alternative bands make. Alternative bands, like postmodern artists in other media, take accepted norms and twist them, referring to the past, mixing high art and low art, creating something accessible that addresses their audience's (and the band's own) issues. For most alternative bands — for virtually all the bands I've examined — that twist of norms is musically violent: Bands hacking away at conventional pop structures, via feedback or bed-of-nails vocals or earthy lyrics or whatever. For the Cocteau Twins, the twist is gentle and elegant, but it's equally alternative, and so equally postmodern. And the twist has paved the way for a slew of hazy, lethargic-sounding bands such as Mazzy Star, Codeine, and Red House Painters, who shuffle instead of scream. They, after so many albums of revved-up guitar, are as cathartic for your ears as a night of moshing to a sixteen-year-old Nirvana fan.

EIGHT

INDUSTRIAL, GOTH, AND OTHER SUB-GENRES

In breaking down the alternative realm into genres—British and American guitar bands, miasma bands, grebo bands, and so on—it should be clear that "alternative" is about as specific an appellation as "rock 'n' roll." I've highlighted specific submovements like "grebo" and "art bands" because of their long-term importance as much on a cultural level as a musical one. Just as one can look back at the musical influence and social frenzy the Beatles created in 1963–1964, people may remember the impact of bands like Nirvana and Jesus and Mary Chain in thirty years' time.

Nonetheless, there are a handful of other bands and alternative subgenres that deserve some attention, at least in passing. I mention them with an eye toward overview instead of with the scrutiny of a close-up lens. While genres like industrial music (which is epitomized by the work of bands like Nine Inch Nails and Ministry), techno, and the synth-pop of bands like Depeche Mode operate in the alternative realm both musically and in terms of audience reaction, the music itself doesn't have the lasting power of albums like My Bloody Valentine's *Isn't Anything* or the Jesus and Mary Chain's *Psychocandy*.

Many acts in this jumble of bands offer their young, lonely, and disenfranchised fans the same oasis of cathartic escape as, say, American guitar bands or miasmic bands do. Perhaps the clearest example is the industrial movement. Industrial music—exemplified by Chicago's Ministry, Cleveland, Ohio's Nine Inch Nails, Revolting Cocks, Front 242, Skinny Puppy—is a gory, sinister combination of throbbing sample-heavy keyboards, evil, cackling vocals, sometimes-bordering-on-metal guitars, and a pounded-out beat that clinks away like a Chinese water torture drip. Members of industrial bands—and their fans—wear black clothes, often in shreds, sometimes integrating studs or leather, or big black Doc Marten boots. They often have almost-ritualistic multiply pierced ears, noses, and (in some cases) nipples, and—as common on men as women—often ring their eyes in chalky black eyeliner. It's the *Cabinet of Dr. Caligari* updated, set to music, and shoved into a dingy club in middle America.

Those clothes are as apocalyptic as the music, which is uniform in its almost macabre darkness. And live—when it's at its most intense—it feels like a set on a sci-fi movie. Ministry, one of the most successful industrial bands, fronts the stage with a black wire fence. Nine Inch Nails leaves chains, unraveled recording tape—which sometimes wraps up lead singer Trent Reznor—and debris cluttered around its stage like a pile of overturned garbage strewn across the ground. The audience takes violent moshing to a frightening extreme. Industrial gigs by the likes of Ministry, the Revolting Cocks, and Nine Inch Nails feel like a stroll through Hell, circa late eighties. It's no wonder that when band order was being assigned for the 1992 Lollapolooza tour, Ministry insisted it play at night.

As grim as it may sound, industrial bands have huge followings and sell vast amounts of records, as the entry of Nine Inch Nails' first release after its debut album, *Pretty Hate Machine*—1992's *Broken* EP—straight into the Billboard top ten chart proves. For me, these bands are more interesting on a cultural level than a musical one. They speak to these kids, attracting huge middle American audiences, by actualizing, visually as well as musically, pure, unadulterated rage. In a sense, this is exactly what Nirvana does, but it is

Nine Inch Nails' Trent Renzor

expressed *differently*, with a *different* look and sound to a *different* audience. But while bands like Nirvana offer a no-frills release of frustration and anger, industrial bands exaggerate that rage and the expression of it. On record, live, in videos, via what they and their fans wear, they enlarge that anger, "theatricalize" it, blow it up until it's unavoidable. They turn common emotions into a scene from *Blade Runner*. Which is, for some fans, the ultimate distillation of internalized feelings (fury, hate, up-against-the-wall frustration) and the mechanization of the outside world via samples and synths, the — hey! postmodern — mix of techno beats and spiky guitars.

Industrial lyrics are as grim as the music they accompany. Nine Inch Nails' debut album, *Pretty Hate Machine*, speaks for itself. It features songs like "Head Like a Hole" (sample choric lyric: "Black as your soul/I'd rather die than give you control/Bow down before the one you serve/you're going to get what you deserve"). Other songs are focused around desperate, "get me out" cries. In "Terrible Lie," Reznor pleads, "Hey God, why are you doing this to me?" In "Sanctified," he sings, "It's still getting worse after everything I tried." Ministry has given its albums sanguineous titles like "The Land of Rape and Honey" and "The Mind is a Terrible Thing to Taste." For

Skinny Puppy, an industrial band from Vancouver, Canada, the postapocalyptic maneuvering of language begins with the band members' names: one member is called Nivek Ogre (or just Ogre to his fans); another cEVIN Key (sic). These bands live in a dark hyperreality that they re-create at their nuclear-doomsday-live shows. At these gigs, hundreds and hundreds of kids swathed in black throw themselves at each other while a snarling band of manic musicians pounds through too-loud beats. Basically, it's a living, breathing nightmare. But it is a nightmare in which kids feel part of a community of like-minded souls, no matter how depressed those souls are. Through their grim clothes and behavior, industrial bands and fans alike can release the same feelings of angst that are expressed in the work of the Smiths, Nirvana, the Wedding Present, as well as Sylvia Plath, Anne Sexton, and Robert Lowell.

If you think that music this dark has a limited appeal, you're wrong. Nine Inch Nails' debut album, *Pretty Hate Machine*, was awarded a gold record in America, which is a particularly noteworthy feat because it came out on an independent label with no track record for working with that kind of music, TVT Records.* Grim industrial lyrics and dark instrumentation address a specific type of fan with painful poignancy. The typical industrial kid is usually white, disenfranchised, and male. On paper, at least, it sounds like the same demographic as the core Nirvana fans, but these kids have a more dramatic, less rootsy taste in music and gig-wear. The success of industrial music in "America's heartland"—a "heartland" filled with strip malls and drive-thru fast food—is no coincidence. Bands like Nine Inch Nails and Ministry—both of whose lead singers have, incidentally, become alternative icons along the lines of Sonic Youth's Kim Gordon and Thurston Moore or Dinosaur Jr.'s J Mascis—speak directly, almost as if by bible verse, to kids who feel trapped, bored, at a dead end. Live and on record, their grim music simultaneously offers empathy and escape.

The initial releases by the Revolting Cocks, Ministry, and Front 242 were all on a Chicago-based indie called Wax Trax. Like the British indie Rough Trade, Wax Trax grew out of a record store, which still exists today. Although many Wax Trax bands are now on

* Although the only indie labels I've discussed specialize in alternative music, there are other independent labels that release only rap, dance, reggae, or any of a number of other genres. TVT actually stands for Tee Vee Toons—the label's initial releases were compilations of commercial jingles and television theme songs.

major labels (Ministry is on Warner Brothers–owned Sire and Front 242 is on Epic), the initial support of the local indie record shop and label proved vital to these bands' careers. Like many cities and towns in America, Chicago has a cool record store (Wax Trax), an indie label of the same name operated with its support, a cool radio station (WHPK-FM, although there are plenty of good college stations there), colleges (like the University of Chicago, Northeastern Illinois, and Northwestern, in nearby Evanston), and a cool club (Cabaret Metro). And like, say, Seattle, Washington, Chicago also has a lot of bored, angry kids whose concerns aren't being addressed by mainstream music – and Chicago has a scene that focuses around the dark, desperate sounds of industrial music.

Just as bands like the Jesus and Mary Chain layer angry noise over a pop-song base, there are, for some industrial bands, pop conventions buried beneath the gore. Nine Inch Nails' "Head Like a Hole" and "Down in It" have pop-song hooks as their foundation. Ministry's first album, *With Sympathy* (released on Arista in 1983), featuring tracks like "Work for Love" and "Cold Life," is straight-ahead techno-pop. But while the Mary Chain or Nirvana are about the mix of aggressive guitar noise with conventional pop antecedents, bands like Ministry (circa 1988–1989, when its albums *The Land of Rape and Honey* and *The Mind Is a Terrible Thing to Taste* were released), Nine Inch Nails (after its *Pretty Hate Machine* album came out in 1989), Front 242, and the Revolting Cocks – are more about rage than pop melodies. Whereas the bands who influenced many of the movements discussed in this book – the Stooges, the Velvet Underground – used a catchy song as part of their musical mix, many industrial influences – like somber, Teutonic electro-futurists Can and the British hyperpercussive band Test Department – are focused more on an overall sound than a pop hook. That structure makes most industrial music seem ephemeral, more about an energy than long-lasting musicality. In other words, an evening at an industrial gig is probably more interesting, in the long run, than listening to a stack of industrial CDs again and again through a set of headphones.

The grim, Addams-Family-come-to-life look that industrial fans have adopted is similar to the style prevalent among the members of another genre of alternative band and their fans: gothic bands. Seminal gothic bands like Bauhaus and Sisters of Mercy were most active in the early and mid-eighties, respectively, predating the industrial movement. Gothic bands offer a similarly dark view of things, although their music doesn't have the apocalyptic, threatening feel of industrial bands. While industrial bands see living in the late twentieth century as living in a coffin, so-called "goth" bands revel in the coffin itself, making music that seems, at its worse, like funeral music gone awry. Actually, it's more like a modern-day *Bride of Frankenstein* soundtrack than industrial's high-tech boom. As industrial music chugs through synthesized gnarl, goth music focuses more on morose singers and rain-cloud-atmospheric melodies. And the horror film analogy is apt: Footage of Bauhaus performing their early single "Bela Lagosi's Dead" opens up the Catherine Deneuve/David Bowie film *The Hunger*. Similarly, goths — as the fans of these bands are called — wear black clothes and eyeliner. While the fashion vibe for industrial fans is violent, twentieth-century apocalypse, goth vibes are somewhat softer — more about wrist-slitting gloom than aggression. In England, America, Germany, and elsewhere, goth music attracts large numbers of female fans, while industrial music does not. It makes sense, as goth lacks industrial's violence but retains its sense of blown-up-adolescent depression.

While industrial bands are fueled by anger, goth bands are driven by almost morbid despair — goth doesn't bite like industrial. Moreover, singers like Bauhaus' Peter Murphy, Sisters of Mercy's Andrew Eldritch, and the Mission's Wayne Hussey (all of whom are goth icons) are heavily influenced by the smooth flamboyance of David Bowie. This influence can be seen in the vocal styles of these singers as well in their larger-than-life stage presence. Bauhaus went so far as to do a true-to-the-original cover of "Ziggy Stardust" to show their Bowie debt. The rooting in Bowiesque vocals and theatrics gives goth music an elegance that industrial bands simply don't have.

The goth movement has affected a few mini-generations of kids. Bauhaus' first EP (featuring "Bela Lagosi's Dead") came out in 1979 and, although the band broke up 1983, there are still plenty of Bauhaus t-shirts on kids from Melrose in L.A. to St. Mark's Place in New York to Berlin. In addition, former lead singer Peter Murphy has had a successful solo career on the band's coattails. The band Love and Rockets, formed by ex–Bauhaus members David J and Daniel Ash, eventually had a huge international hit with the single "So Alive."

There's also an apocalyptic quality to the Pixies, an American band of great importance, that touches on several of the genres but doesn't fit fully into any one. The Pixies are as loud and shake-it-out-of-you guitar-focused as Dinosaur Jr., as no-bullshit as Nirvana, and feature moments of feedback somewhat reminiscent of Jesus and Mary Chain. In fact, the band covered the Mary Chain's "Head On" on its final *Trompe Le Monde* LP, in 1991. Before the band broke up, it was on art band–based 4AD Records, which licenses the band to Time Warner–owned Elektra Records in America. And the Pixies' songs feature the sort of bizarre avant-poetic lyrics that macabre, American Mark E. Smith might write. In a sense, the Pixies are a handful of alternative subgenres rolled into one. And although their success has been virtually entirely in the alternative realm in America, in Europe they've had the success of a thousand alternative bands, playing huge venues and selling loads of records.

Seeing them live, you'd think they were some sort of rock 'n' roll evangelists: Kids go farther than the moshing and stage diving they'd do at a Nirvana or Dinosaur Jr. gig. They chant religiously along with the band's lyrics, which are not exactly singalong ditties, as mere titles like "Wave of Mutilation," "Break My Body," and "Gouge My Body" show. The kids move in huge waves, which, if you're watching from an overhead balcony, look like an aerial shot of some perverse, choreographed, synchronized swimming. Just as there's something frightening and surreal about kids singing along to Morrissey's "I want to kill myself" lyrics or, to pull an example from a different bunch of fans, to Ice-T's "Cop Killer," that intense devotion to a band whose t-shirts read "Death to the Pixies" is a bit macabre. Then again, sixteen-year-old kids having to deal with AIDS and drug addiction and teenage pregnancy and anorexia has a macabre ring to it as well. Unquestionably, other bands have devoted fans who sing along and dance, but for the Pixies, that adoration seems extra-pious, almost blindly religious. The difference between the Pixies' "fan-dom" and that of any other band is the difference between a monastery-bound monk and a Sunday-only churchgoer.

But if you take their song titles and t-shirt slogans seriously you're missing the point: The band is equal parts rock 'n' roll and surrealism. It's almost too obvious to quote the lyrics of "Debaser," a quirked-out tribute to Salvador Dali. As evidence: "slicing up eyeballs/I want you to know," along with a screamed, cackling chorus, "I am un chien andalusia." Both allusions are to Dali's surrealist classic. Many of the band's lyrics—like "Is She Weird's" "your heart is ripshit/your mouth is everywhere/I'm lyin in it!" and "Monkey's

The Pixies' Black Francis

Gone to Heaven's" "there was a guy/an under water guy who controlled the sea/got killed by ten million pounds of sludge/from New York and New Jersey"—share the tone of surrealist photographs such as May Ray's famous *Violon d'Ingres* (a turban-topped woman, back to the lens, with drawn holes transforming her torso into a violin) or *L'Enigme d'Isidore Ducasse* (a picture of a later-destroyed sewing machine wrapped in burlap and rope so it looks unidentifiable but almost like an entrapped body). Strange and slightly sick, these photos, like the Pixies' tracks, elicit initial shock and then – if you get it – sinister, curdling laughter. The band's vocals simply add to that surreality. Black Francis's voice is alternately a monkey squawk, ballsy scream, obscene phone call pant, crooner's voice, and evil howl. Kim Deal's mock-vulnerable, little-girl-lost-gone-bad peep is equally captivating. Both vocalists are somehow jubilant and dark at the same time.

Nonetheless, the most appropriate analogy for the Pixies' music may be a night of schlock television: equal parts spaghetti western (tracks like *Surfer Rosa*'s "Cactus" and *Doolittle*'s "Mr. Grieves"), lightweight situation comedy (*Bossanova*'s "Alison" and *Doolittle*'s "Here Comes Your Man"), the Spanish-speaking network, where occasionally you understand the few words of English thrown in (*Surfer Rosa*'s "Oh My Golly!" and "I'm Amazed"), plus something for the kids ("U. Mass," off *Trompe le Monde*), and something scary and violent (like "Wave of Mutilation").

Certainly, there are those many dimensions in the Pixies' music, but – like the Jesus and Mary Chain, like Nirvana – the band often takes conventional pop structures and melodies and twists them. With something for listeners beyond the alternative realm to latch on to – like the singsong choruses of "Gigantic," "Here Comes Your Man," and "Monkey Gone to Heaven" and the sweet melodies in "Wave of Mutilation" and "Alec Eiffel" – you wonder, with such firmly hooky choruses to those songs, why they were never bigger in America. All these songs have the sort of classic pop hooks that, even juxtaposed with weird lyrics, would seem to make them obvious hit material. With these anthemic, memorable songs, one would think that the Pixies should have been able to reach beyond alternative systems like a Nirvana did with "Smells Like Teen Spirit." Then again, Nirvana's huge success had to do with timing, cultural currents (i.e., the recession of the early nineties in full swing), promotion, label commitment, and, to be fair, some luck as well. The point is that both bands build on a pop-song base – more so than the more wandering songs of the Cocteau Twins or My Bloody Valentine – and clink away at that base in an alternative and thus postmodern way.

Fugazi, from Washington, D.C., shares the Pixies' dark, angry churn. But the way Fugazi vents it comes out differently. Led by Ian MacKaye, the band's focal point is its seething, chunked-up guitars, which sound like they're about to burst. In a sense, the band's guitar sound is sort of the American hardcore-influenced version of the guitars that drive Mega City Four. The analogy makes sense, since MacKaye was in the seminal hardcore band Minor Threat. Fugazi's throttled energy attracts a specific fan: young, usually male, politically aware. The typical Fugazi fan wears a cleaned-up, skinhead or nearly skinhead version of grungewear featuring thrift-store clothes washed and tucked in, big sturdy shoes, no-frills t-shirts. These fans are devoutly into Fugazi. The band's shows are full of slamming and anger. Its trademark guitars — you can imagine a band like Wire gone schitzoid or the Gang of Four at an L.A. riot — express and direct that anger, offering a cathartic release for its fans in the way that Sonic Youth and Dinosaur Jr. do. It's no wonder so many of its fans are teenaged. Musically, what Fugazi does replicates an adolescent temper tantrum, shaking and screaming, bursting with rage.

But Fugazi is important for more than just its music. Alternative bands work within their own systems. They reject and personalize conventional musical norms, not just in the way their music sounds but in the way it is released and promoted. To circulate that music, alternative bands use their own network of college radio stations, clubs, magazines, distribution. Fugazi leader Ian MacKaye runs the band's indie label, provocatively called Dischord. Part of the goal of the label is to release local bands, all of whom seem to have a coherent grind at their core. Dischord bands like Lungfish, the now-defunct Nation of Ulysses, and Shudder to Think all layer their own elements (Shudder's wild vocals and almost-jazz turns and Nation Of's manifesto rants) on top of that guitar rage. Remarkably, its albums now sell in the 200,000-copy range in America alone, which would be excellent sales for an alternative band on a major label with major promotion, distribution, tour support, and staffing. On an indie, with a staff of a handful, it's incredible. Fugazi not only won't bump up to a major like Nirvana did but it distributes its releases — all Dischord releases, for that matter — at a special low price. Although its live reputation is part of what's gotten it this far, the band will only do gigs where ticket prices are kept low. In an age of mega-profit and mark-ups, Fugazi offers an accessible alternative, which is, of course, what they do musically as well. For his firm commitment to these sorts of ideals, MacKaye has become as much of an alternative icon as Sonic Youth's Kim Gordon and Thurston Moore.

But Fugazi isn't the only band to run a label, support its local bands, and set its releases at affordable prices: Two other D.C. natives have done the same thing. Mark Robinson, who fronts the band

Unrest, runs a label called TeenBeat, which features Eggs, Jonny Cohen, and others in addition to his own band; the label presents its releases in some of the most inventive grass-roots packaging around. Jenny Toomey runs Simple Machines, which releases music by her band, Tsunami, as well as others. And there are other examples: Two members of the band Superchunk run Merge; Beat Happening runs K Records in its home state of Washington. Even Sonic Youth has a label for local bands, Ecstatic Peace, although some of its releases, by bands like Cell and St. Johnny, now go through Geffen. In the same way that the clichéd image of label-president-as-big-bad-businessman is broken by 4AD's Ivo Watts-Russell and Creation's Alan McGee, who periodically release their own bands' music, the standard record industry system is subverted by bands that run their own labels. The myth of rock stars as unaware or uninvolved in their business lives, killing time with groupies and drugs, is thus dispelled. Musicians like Ian MacKaye and Mark Robinson run their own labels on their own terms, focus on music over profit, and have 100 percent control over their careers. In other words, these musicians flip major-label standards on their sides. But for the hundreds of thousands of kids who just aren't adequately addressed by the major-label ethic (big business and corporate bottom line versus the sensibility of small labels run with microscopic staffs), that flip rules.

In addition to musician-run labels, there are plenty of American, seven-inch-only labels, like Pop Narcotic, Slumberland, Funky Mushroom, Dark Beloved Cloud, and so many others. These are run on a similarly sparse level, but, by addressing the pinpointable "indie kid" demographic—the ones moshing at Dinosaur Jr. shows, the ones nodding along to My Bloody Valentine (even though both are now on major labels)—they do survive. Frequently, these labels release local bands' music, which makes perfect sense. They're an extension of the college radio station/local fanzine/cool clothing shop and book shop/alternative record shop network. By supporting a local scene, as Dischord does with its D.C.-based roster, these labels support themselves. To a similar end, the Providence, Rhode Island, band small factory promoted a festival of East Coast indie bands in 1992 called "Indie Rock Ain't Noise Pollution," modeled after a similar gathering organized by K Records in Olympia, Washington, in 1991. These support systems allow labels, bands, and fans to work together and survive. But most of the labels were started with out-of-pocket funds and exist only to release uncompromising music.

The same support happens halfway around the world in New

Zealand on the Flying Nun label. Although it may not seem like a cultural capital, New Zealand has spawned a handful of bands which share an expansive sound: the Chills, the Straitjacket Fits, the 3D's, the Clean, the Tall Dwarfs, Bailter Space, the Bats. These bands have all released records on the indie Flying Nun; in addition, their members, in the share-a-pint-of-Foster's spirit of things, frequently bounce between bands, spending stints in them all. These bands aren't soundalike similar. The Chills sound like an aural wide-angle shot of a mountaintop on *Submarine Bells*, which was licensed to Slash-Warner Brothers in 1990. The Straitjacket Fits are booming, atmospheric mood-guitar-pop. The Clean are even poppier, and the 3D's jangle with taut guitars. Despite their differences, all these bands embody the local-indie-support-local-scene ethic as poignantly as Dischord bands do. They also exemplify the alternative strategy of taking a pop-song foundation and twisting that base with personal flair. Key examples of this technique include the Chills' cheeky "Heavenly Pop Hit," the Straitjacket Fits' "Down in Splendour," and "Not Given Lightly" by Chris Knox, half of the Tall Dwarfs. The first of these songs has all-encompassing breadth, the second has the somber mahogany layers that are the key to the Straitjackets' sound, and the third chirps along with a charming, underproduced, basement quality. In America, a few of the New Zealand bands have been picked up by major labels, but clearly they're not huge successes. Nonetheless, they have all garnered the kind of critical acclaim and small, hipster audiences that indicate, if not necessarily future success, at least future influence.

Perhaps the clearest pre-Nirvana example of an alternative band's growing beyond its original base is R.E.M., which is also a product of a local, supportive scene: Athens, Georgia, circa 1981. Out of the scene focused around the University of Georgia and its accompanying alternative music systems—the college radio station, WUOG-FM, the cool club (Tyrone's when the band was forming, the 40 Watt Club now), cheap clothing, and bookstores—R.E.M., the B-52's, Pylon, and several other seminal alternative bands got their start. Although the band is now on Warner Brothers and huge around the world—and was on mid-sized label IRS before that—R.E.M.'s first single came out on a small local label and was propelled by local support. Similarly, it was the support of Seattle-based SubPop, radio station KCMU, clubs like Backstage, and record shops like Fallout which gave Nirvana—along with Pearl Jam, Mudhoney, Screaming Trees—its first fan bases.

Musically, R.E.M. does twist pop conventions with alternately strange and (more recently) politically correct lyrics, too many, almost too American strummy guitars, and lead singer Michael Stipe's oddball creak of a voice. Breaking the high and low art distinction, the band had the photography duo, the Starn Twins, design the cover art for *Out of Time*. Obviously, that pair's work usually hangs in galleries instead of record racks. The band makes consistently arty videos, which look sometimes like a Stan Brakhage film ("Driver 8"), sometimes like a hip Pierre Et Gilles hyper-color, hokey-posed photograph ("Losing My Religion"), and sometimes like a black-and-white Bruce Weber montage ("Drive"). Playing Madison Square Garden, winning Grammys, being repeatedly on the cover of *Rolling Stone*, R.E.M. has bounded into the mainstream with little compromise of their original direction.

All of which would lead one to believe that the band should have a whole chapter in this book, but to me it just doesn't make the same kinds of musical innovations that other important alternative bands do. Certainly, R.E.M. is no Madonna—but, then again, it's no My Bloody Valentine, either. In a sense, it's like a yuppie alternative: sort of mellow, fine on a home stereo, cool but not frightening, jangly in a very American way. And so, to me, the band is not all that interesting on a musical or cultural level.

And speaking of cultural levels, it could easily be said that Depeche Mode is more interesting from that angle than from a musical one. Case in point: In the documentary film of its U.S. tour, *101*, directed by D. A. Pennebacker, the most interesting segments focus on the fans. Dressed somewhere between goth and industrial fans, mostly female, explaining their practically religious alliance to the band, Depeche fans are die-hard and numerous. Along with the Cure, Depeche Mode is king of commercial alternative radio. It is safer and sweeter than many of the bands I've focused on in depth (even if the members do play with sexual/sadomasochistic imagery by wearing black leather and singing songs like "Master and Servant" and "Personal Jesus," and even if there is a superficial darkness to the sound). By simply adding a synthesizer, a heavy beat, and Bowie-influenced vocals over what are standard pop songs, the band is basically an electro-pop band dressed in black. Bubble-gum alternative, if you will. So although the band also plays stadiums in America, has had huge success, and twists pop conventions like so many other alternative bands do, it doesn't have the musical sophistication of Sonic Youth or the Cocteau Twins.

The same could be said of the Cure. There's something almost surreal about the band. For a start, the band's frontman, Robert Smith, with his Brillo-pad hair and smudged red lipstick, looks more like a Saturday morning cartoon character than a cool lead singer. While the band's records consistently make their way into the top ten of the American album sales chart, its members still look weird and sound quite different from the other bands on the charts. Although the band has lost its initial angry-young-man jolt, it has stayed close to the general direction of early tracks like "Boys Don't Cry" and "Killing an Arab," which were released in 1980 on the American *Boys Don't Cry* LP. Like Depeche Mode, its alternative airplay is now predominantly on big, safe, commercial alternative stations. Both bands get mainstream airplay on radio and MTV, and although they are still often labeled alternative, work mostly within more conventional systems. Bands like the Cure and Depeche Mode twist accepted musical norms in slighter, subtler ways than bands like Sonic Youth do and don't have the latter's earth-shattering impact.

Yet Depeche Mode and the Cure both started on small labels (Mute and Fiction, respectively), both built a base through the support of fanzines and small record shops and college radio stations. Certainly, both bands sound less shocking on mainstream radio than, say, an industrial band, or even Nirvana, would. And both use the formula of twisting a standard pop base. But the key difference between a band like Nirvana and one like Depeche Mode is that, while the latter always cleaned up its edges to attract an increasing number of people, Nirvana still leaves all the warts in its sound. By daring its fans to understand, the band educates fans to like more than bland, easy-to-digest, typical top-40 hits.

And so, it may sound more academic than it is in reality, but one of the goals of the alternative movement, which it shares with postmodern literature, dance, and film, is to get fans to think and be aware. And that goal is missing from the bulk of the bands discussed in this chapter. Industrial bands and goth bands are simply about a (usually transient) sound. They simply don't call upon their fans to open their minds and think about their world, and thus they lack the depth that other alternative subgenres have.

CONCLUSION

NINE

Having established not only that the alternative realm exists but that many of its bands can be clumped into musical and cultural sub-genres, the question remains as to why alternative music is so important. It's all well and good that alternative music resonates toward an overall definition of postmodernism — but its importance has to relate to more than theory.

The answer comes in several parts. First of all, the sheer number of alternative fans makes it an important movement. Unquestionably, many people bought, heard, and enjoyed Nirvana's "Smells Like Teen Spirit" single who are not alternative fans and never will be. As a number-one song on charts around the world, that single has often been played before and after safe, glistening pop radio fare featuring all the well-produced musical norms Nirvana so emphatically tries to negate. But if the fans of grebo, miasma, American and British guitar bands, art bands, and the other subgenres were to be added up, the numbers would get very large. The commercial success of an alternative music festival like Lollapolooza shows just how big those numbers are.

Yet the mere fact that Nirvana's single infiltrated itself onto mainstream radio is telling. Sure, its crystal-clear pop line got it there, but, lodged into playlists, the single woke listeners up, making the more mainstream bands it was played beside seem almost obsolete. In other words, by reproportioning vocals or feedback to guitar noise, Nirvana, like other alternative bands, compels listeners to question more "standard" pop music. Simply put, Nirvana played back to back with Whitney Houston makes the latter sound as off-kilter as Sonic Youth's guitar tunings do. And so listeners are forced to think—something top-40 radio doesn't exactly encourage.

On a musical level, alternative bands are breaking new ground. But they are also borrowing old rock 'n' roll structures and twisting them. It's important to note that the underlying core out of which most alternative bands burst was formed by white musicians instead of black ones. In the sixties, bands like the Beatles and the Rolling Stones were influenced by black artists like Little Richard and Chuck Berry. On the contrary, bands like Sonic Youth and Kitchens of Distinction spring off a base of, well, the Beatles and the Stones, as well as other white guitar bands like the Velvet Underground. Like an old wives' tale passed down from generation to generation, most alternative bands are one step further away from rock 'n' roll's roots than its predecessors were. Even a band like the Jesus and Mary Chain, which is so clearly bound to sixties music, is influenced by sixties bands like the Beach Boys and girl groups that Phil Spector worked with. And one very influential alternative band from the seventies, Big Star, laid a white power pop foundation for bands like the Replacements, Teenage Fanclub, and the GooGoo Dolls. The rooting of the alternative scene in white guitar bands does not lead to a big racial conclusion, but it does highlight a pronounced difference between these bands and some of their antecedents.

Culturally, "alternative" is a movement of action. The politically aware lyrics of a band like Sonic Youth, and the declared radicalism of a submovement like the Riot Grrrls, demonstrate this aspect of the music. It's music for a generation of kids who are politically aware and socially conscious. It's also music for a generation that uses that music to violently—*actively*—jolt them into both a release from and a confrontation with their problems. Sonically, miasma bands and feedback bands force listeners to deal with and think about the confusion of their world. They respond to their surroundings through both music and lyrics.

These bands also ask listeners to question their own concepts of beauty. With its unique images of beauty—like, say, the guitar angst of the Wedding Present—the alternative scene offers its specific vision to specific fans. Role models like Kim Gordon and Mark E. Smith offer a new counterculture image to kids whose parents, former hippies, already tuned in and dropped out. Growing up with AIDS and homelessness in their world, the bite of this music not only makes it relevant but makes all other music seem irrelevant.

The social echoes of alternative music do not take in the whole picture, however. The definition of alternative music as postmodern is also vital. Like any other postmodern artist, Nirvana tips its hat to the past and then somehow rips that hat in two. (In Nirvana's case, this means chugging Beatlesque melodies through a throatful of nails.) Sure, Nirvana now has some top-40 smashes, but what makes Nirvana different from the other artists on the top-40 chart is that its music maintains its angry bite and fuck-the-mainstream anticommerciality. By breaking the borders of mainstream versus alternative, the band has made, in some ways, parallels between high art and low art. Nirvana universalizes something that was formerly available to just a select few. Except that the select who made up Nirvana's initial fan base were hardly snooty museum-goers. They were flannel-shirted kids bored and pissed off, getting drunk in grimy clubs. The Metropolitan Museum of Art, alternative clubs sure ain't.

Those flannel shirts have come to be worn on runways around the world, and Nirvana's music sells millions of copies. Alternative music is not just cool. It fills a need for a generation of kids who are bored and alienated. Like punk rock before it, alternative music initially scared off some of the fans it has now won. But truly alternative bands continually aim to broaden their scope, to remain daring.

And like punk—and Situationism and Dada and graffiti art—alternative music is an accessible art. Its venues are sweaty clubs and crammed little record shops and low-fi college radio stations. If, as Gil Scott Heron wrote, "the revolution must be televised," the alternative music revolution must be broadcast and blared and yelled off stages across the country. And that's exactly what kids are doing.

And those kids aren't going anywhere. Alternative magazines

like *Alternative Press* and fashion accessories like flannel shirts and Doctor Marten boots have grown in popularity just as Nirvana's music has. And so alternative music may wave at the past, but it points at the present and toward the future. As an expression of how a generation feels about that present and future, it's undeniably important.

DISCOGRAPHY

The following record list is not meant to be all-inclusive; however, it is a representative shopping list for the key records discussed in the text. If you need a soundtrack by which to read, this is it:

MIASMA BANDS

MY BLOODY VALENTINE
"Sunny Sundae Smile" EP (Lazy import)
"Feed Me With Your Kiss" EP (Creation import)
"You Made Me Realize" EP (Creation import)
Ecstasy and Wine LP (Lazy import)
Isn't Anything LP (Sire)
Glider EP (Sire)
Tremolo EP (Sire)
Loveless (Sire)

In a sense, *Isn't Anything* and *Loveless* are the keys to miasma music – although the band's EPs are also required listening. *Ecstasy and Wine* is a collection of pre-miasmic singles; the band's sound prior to that can be heard on a hard-to-find collection called *This Is Your Bloody Valentine*, released by a German label called Dossier.

THE BOO RADLEYS
Everything's Alright Forever LP (Columbia)
Boo! Forever EP (Columbia)
Lazarus EP (Creation import)

The Boos are the miasma band with the most long-term potential. Also worth checking out are the band's pre-LP singles, like the smashing "Finest Kiss," available as Rough Trade imports.

CATHERINE WHEEL
Ferment LP (Mercury)

CURVE
Doppelganger LP (Charisma)
Pubic Fruit EP (Charisma)

LUSH
Gala LP (4AD-Reprise)
Spooky LP (4AD-Reprise)

RIDE
Nowhere LP (Sire)
Going Blank Again LP (Sire)

SLOWDIVE
Just for a Day LP (SBK)

SWERVEDRIVER
Raise LP (A&M)

For background listening, the most essential band is the Velvet Underground. The band's first three albums, all available on Verve — *The Velvet Underground & Nico*, *White Light/White Heat*, and *The Velvet Underground* — are all miasma classics. More recent influences include A.R. Kane (best compiled on an American Luaka Bop LP, *Americana*) and Galaxie 500 (with Rough Trade LPs *On Fire* and *This Is Our Music*).

BRITISH GUITAR BANDS

THE SMITHS
The Smiths LP (Sire)
Hatful of Hollow LP (Rough Trade import)
Meat Is Murder LP (Sire)
The Queen Is Dead LP (Sire)
Strangeways, Here We Come LP (Sire)
Best . . . I LP (Sire)
Best . . . II LP (Sire)

Although the band's greatest-hits compilations capture its mix of melodrama, angst, and impassioned jangle, *The Smiths*, *Meat Is Mur-*

der, and *The Queen Is Dead* are probably the best examples of the band at its prime.

THE FALL
Perverted By Language LP (Rough Trade import)
The Frenz Experiment LP (Big Time)
Extricate LP (Fontana import)
The Infotainment Scam LP (Matador/Atlantic)

There are far more Fall LPs than are listed—but these provide a sample of the band's choppy sound.

KITCHENS OF DISTINCTION
Love Is Hell LP (originally released in America on Rough Trade; reissued by A&M)
Strange Free World LP (A&M)
The Death of Cool LP (A&M)

THE WEDDING PRESENT
George Best LP (Reception import)
Bizarro LP (RCA)
Sea Monsters LP (RCA)
Hit Parade 1 LP (First Warning)
Hit Parade 2 LP (RCA import)

While all these album show off the mile-a-minute sound of the band, it's worth tracking down the Wedding Present's many import singles, since they often include non-LP tracks.

THE CHAMELEONS
Strange Times LP (Geffen)

WIRE
Pink Flag LP (Restless Retro)
Chairs Missing LP (Restless Retro)

These are both seminal British guitar albums which were hugely influential to bands like the Smiths and the Wedding Present.

THE BUZZCOCKS
Spiral Scratch EP (New Hormones import)
A Different Kind of Tension LP (I.R.S.)

Singles Going Steady LP (IRS)

The Buzzcocks are, along with Wire, the direct catalyst for British guitar bands.

Other releases which have influenced the British guitar school include Television's *Marquee Moon* LP (Elektra) and David Bowie's *Ziggy Stardust and the Spiders from Mars* LP (Rykodisc). There are many more recent bands which follow in the jangly footsteps of British guitar bands. Records worth checking out are: Pavement's *Slanted and Enchanted* LP (Matador), Unrest's *Malcolm X Park* LP (Caroline), and Suede's self-titled debut LP (nude-Columbia).

AMERICAN GUITAR BANDS

DINOSAUR JR
You're Living All Over Me LP (SST)
Bug LP (SST)
Just Like Heaven EP (SST)
Green Mind LP (Sire)
Whatever's Cool with Me LP (Sire)
Where You Been LP (Sire)

In a sense, *the* American guitar band. Play loud.

SONIC YOUTH
Bad Moon Rising LP (Homestead)
Evol LP (SST)
Sister LP (SST)
Daydream Nation LP (Blast First)
Goo LP (DGC)
Dirty LP (DGC)

In addition to these hugely influential albums, it's worth checking out the album the band did with fIREHOSE's Mike Watt: *The Whitey Album*, released under the band name Ciccone Youth by Blast First in 1989.

NIRVANA
"Bleach" LP (SubPop)
Nevermind LP (DGC)
Incesticide LP (DGC)

Of course, *Nevermind* introduced Nirvana—and American guitar music as a whole—to most people, but *"Bleach"* also has some great moments.

Of the scores of bands influenced by these three, here are the most noteworthy:

IN THE DINOSAUR JR. VEIN

BUFFALO TOM
Birdbrain LP (Beggar's Banquet)
Let Me Come Over LP (Beggar's Banquet)

LEMONHEADS
Lick LP (Taang)
Lovey LP (Atlantic)
Famous Spanish Dishes EP (Atlantic)
It's a Shame About Ray LP (Atlantic)

UNCLE TUPELO
No Depression LP (Rockville)
Still Feel Gone LP (Rockville)

SEBADOH
The Freed Man LP (Homestead)
Smash Your Head On the Punk Rock LP (SubPop)
Bubble and Scrape LP (SubPop)

AFTER NIRVANA

THE AFGHAN WHIGS
Congregation LP (SubPop)
"Conjure Me"/"My World Is Empty Without You" 45 (SubPop)
Uptown Avondale EP (SubPop)

PEARL JAM
Ten LP (Epic)

SOUNDGARDEN
Louder Than Love LP (A&M)
Badmotorfinger LP (A&M)

MUDHONEY

Mudhoney LP (SubPop)
Every Good Boy Deserves Fudge LP (Subpop)
Piece of Cake LP (Reprise)

IN THE SONIC YOUTH TRADITION

L7:

Bricks Are Heavy LP (SubPop)
Pretend We're Dead LP (Slash)

BABES IN TOYLAND

Fontanelle LP (Reprise)

HOLE

Pretty on the Inside LP (Caroline)

The biggest influence on the American guitar school is the Stooges, whose self-titled debut LP (on Elektra) – as well as later albums like *Fun House* (Elektra) and *Raw Power* (Columbia) – is a must-listen. Also important are Neil Young's *Harvest*, *Tonight's the Night*, and the *Decade* compilation, all released by Reprise. A more recent influence is Hüsker Dü, who are best heard on the albums *Metal Circus*, *Zen Arcade*, and *Flip Your Wig*, all on SST. Former Hüsker lead singer Bob Mould's new band, Sugar, has a similar sound, which can be heard on its debut album, *Copper Blue* (Rykodisc).

Worth noting as well is the influence of the California punk movement. Key albums include: the Minutemen's *The Punch Line* and *What Makes a Man Start Fires?* LPs (both on SST), the Dead Kennedys' *Fresh Fruit for Rotting Vegetables* LP (IRS), and Black Flag's *Damaged* LP (SST). Several British bands, all led by women, paved the way for Kim Gordon and the female-driven bands which have since had their ways paved by her. Their most catalystic albums are: X-Ray Spex's *Germ Free Adolescents* LP (Caroline), Au Pairs' *Playing With a Different Sex* (Human Records import), and the Delta 5's *See the Whirl* (Pre).

GREBO BANDS

MEGA CITY FOUR
Tranzophobia LP (Decoy import)
Terribly Sorry Bob LP (Decoy import)
Sebastopol Road LP (Big Life)

Although the Megas are best heard live, these albums epitomize the band's grebo sound.

NED'S ATOMIC DUSTBIN
Bite LP (Chapter 22 import)
God Fodder LP (Columbia)
Are You Normal? LP (Columbia)

THE WONDER STUFF
The Eight Legged Groove Machine LP (Polydor)
HUP LP (Polydor)
Never Loved Elvis LP (Polydor)

JESUS JONES
Liquidizer LP (SBK)
Doubt LP (SBK)

THE SENSELESS THINGS
The First of Too Many LP (Epic)

CARTER THE UNSTOPPABLE SEX MACHINE
101 Damnations LP (Chrysalis)
30 Something LP (Chrysalis)
1992: The Love Album LP (Chrysalis)

POP WILL EAT ITSELF
"Wise Up Sucker" 45 (RCA)
This Is the Day This Is the Hour This Is This! LP (RCA)
Cure For Sanity LP (RCA)

The closest American equivalent to a grebo band is the Red Hot Chili Peppers, as can be heard on albums like *Mother's Milk* (EMI).

FEEDBACK BANDS

THE JESUS AND MARY CHAIN
Psychocandy LP (Reprise)
Darklands LP (Blanco y Negro-Warner Brothers)
Barbed Wire Kisses LP (Blanco y Negro-Warner Brothers)
Automatic LP (Blanco y Negro-Warner Brothers)
Honey's Dead LP (Blanco y Negro-Warner Brothers)

The Jesus and Mary Chain epitomize feedback music. Albums which demonstrate the band's impact include: the Telescopes' *Taste* (What Goes On import) and *Trade Mark of Quality* (Fierce import), Loop's *A Gilded Eternity* (Beggar's Banquet), and Spacemen 3's *The Perfect Prescription* (Genius).

ART BANDS

THE COCTEAU TWINS
Head Over Heels LP (4AD import)
Treasure LP (4AD import)
The Pink Opaque LP (4AD-Relativity)
Victorialand LP (4AD import)
Blue Bell Knoll LP (4AD-Capitol)
Heaven or Las Vegas LP (4AD-Capitol)

As the Jesus and Mary Chain define feedback music, the Cocteau Twins define art music. The Cocteaus' sound resonates on the following releases:

DEAD CAN DANCE
The Serpent's Egg LP (4AD import)
Aion LP (4AD import)

THE SUNDAYS
reading, writing, arithmetic LP (DGC)
Blind LP (DGC)

THIS MORTAL COIL
It'll End in Tears LP (4AD import)
Filigree and Shadow (4AD import)
Blood LP (4AD import)

MAZZY STAR
She Hangs Brightly LP (Capitol)

INDUSTRIAL BANDS

NINE INCH NAILS
Pretty Hate Machine LP (TVT)

MINISTRY
The Land of Rape and Honey LP (Sire)
The Mind Is a Terrible Thing to Taste LP (Sire)

SKINNY PUPPY
Too Dark Park LP (Nettwerk-Capitol)

GOTH BANDS

BAUHAUS
In a Flat Field LP (4AD import)
Mask LP (Beggar's Banquet)

SISTERS OF MERCY
Floodland LP (Elektra)

NEW ZEALAND BANDS

THE CHILLS
Kaleidoscope World LP (Homestead)
Submarine Bells LP (Slash-Warner Brothers)

STRAITJACKET FITS
Hail LP (Rough Trade)
Melt LP (Arista)

OTHER ASSORTED AMERICAN BANDS

THE PIXIES
Come on Pilgrim LP (4AD-Rough Trade)
Surfer Rosa LP (4AD-Rough Trade)
Doolittle LP (4AD-Elektra)

Bossanova LP (4AD-Elektra)
Trompe Le Monde (4AD-Elektra)

FUGAZI
13 Songs LP (Dischord)
Repeater LP (Dischord)

UNREST
Imperial ffrr LP (TeenBeat)

MORE MAINSTREAM ALTERNATIVE BANDS

R.E.M.
Chronic Town EP (IRS)
Murmur LP (IRS)
Reckoning LP (IRS)
Green LP (Warner Brothers)
Out of Time LP (Warner Brothers)
Document LP (Warner Brothers)

DEPECHE MODE
Some Great Reward LP (Mute-Sire)
Black Celebration LP (Mute-Sire)
Violator LP (Mute-Sire-Reprise)
Songs of Faith and Devotion LP (Sire-Reprise)

THE CURE
Boys Don't Cry LP (Fiction-PVC)
Seventeen Seconds LP (Elektra)
The Top LP (Fiction-Sire)
The Head on the Door LP (Elektra)
Disintegration LP (Elektra)

MUSIC GUIDE

An annotated guide to where to hear, buy, and see alternative music in selected American cities – and London:

CHICAGO
Clubs:
Lounge Ax. 2438 N. Lincoln Avenue. 312-525-6620. A small, intimate, back-room-of-the-bar kind of place, it's best when it's packed.

Cabaret Metro. 3730 N. Clark Street. 312-549-0203. Bigger than Lounge Ax, it's the place to see many alternative bands – often on major labels – who reach a slightly bigger audience.

Radio Stations:
WXRT. Your typical, mainstream-end-of-the-alternative spectrum, commercial alternative radio fare.
WNUR: Northwestern's station, based in Evanston. Way cool.

Record Shops:
Wax Trax. 2449 N. Lincoln Avenue. 312-929-0221. Home of the industrial label of the same name, this store stocks loads of techno as well as plenty of other subgenres of the alternative realm.

Reckless. 3157 N. Broadway. 312-404-5080. The most comprehensive alternative store in town, it features a huge selection of magazines, books, imports, and t-shirts as well as domestic singles and CDs.

Local mags to check out: *Chicago Reader, New Times.*

LOS ANGELES
Clubs:

The Whiskey-a-Go-Go. 8901 Sunset Blvd. 310-652-9411. Sort of the CBGB's of L.A., the Whiskey is the cool place to see up-and-coming alternative bands in all their sweaty splendor.

Raji's. 6160 Hollywood Blvd. 213-469-4552. A cool, albeit small place to see new alternative bands.

Bogarts. 6288 East Pacific Coast Highway, Long Beach. 310-594-8975. Although it's a long drive from the center of L.A., it's worth the trip.

Radio Stations:
KUCI. A cool college station with heavy indie airplay.
KCRW: Based in Santa Monica, one of the hippest stations in the country.
KXLU. A varied playlist, but during the alternative slots, it's cool.
KROQ: Standard commercial alternative playlist.

Record Stores:
Aron's. 1150 N Highland. 213-469-4700. Easily the best record shop in L.A, it's the place to get cool alternative stuff.
Record Retreat: 3355 S. Hoover. 213-749-7677.

Local mags: *L.A. Weekly, Ben Is Dead, Flipside, Fiz.*

SAN FRANCISCO
Clubs:
Slim's. 333 11th St. 415-621-3330. Crowded, loud, dark, and sweaty: all an alternative club should be.
DNA Lounge. 375 11th St. 415-626-1409. A busy club which hosts dance parties as well as gigs.

Radio Stations:
KUSF. The hip college station in San Francisco.
KALX: Berkeley's station. Also worth a listen.
Live 105: SF's commercial alternative station.

Record Shops:
Rough Trade. 1529 Haight St. 415-621-4395. Although the label of the same name is now defunct in America, it's name lives on with this cool record shop, featuring an extensive selection, as well as magazines.
Aquarius. 3941 24th Street. 415-647-2272. Another good source for alternative records.

Reckless: 1401 Haight St. 415-431-3434. Also worth checking out, this store is affiliated with the one in Chiacgo.

Mod Lang. 2135 University Ave. 510-486.1880. Although it's out in Berkeley, this shop is highly, highly recommended. While you're there, ask for Mike Shulman, who works there and runs the cool indie Slumberland Records.

Local mags: *SF Weekly, Puncture.*

WASHINGTON, D.C.
Clubs:
The 9:30 Club. 930 F Street Northwest. 202-393-0255. *The* club in D.C., period.

Radio Stations:
WRGW. George Washington University's cool college station.
WHFS: A commercial alternative station servicing D.C. as well as Maryland.

Records Stores:
Vinyl Ink. 995 Bonifant St., Silver Spring, MD. 301-588-4695. A big selection of alternative stuff.
Olsson's. 1239 Wisconsin Ave. N.W. 202-338-6712. More conveniently located, this shop is also good.

Local mags: *City Paper, Chickfactor.*

BOSTON
Clubs:
The Middle East. 472 Massachusetts Ave. 617-492-9181. The Middle East, which is attached to a restaurant specializing in (surprise,

surprise) middle-eastern food, is actually two clubs: a larger down-stairs and a sardine-packed upstairs. A great venue.

T.T. The Bear's. 10 Brookine. 617-492-0082. Around the corner from the Middle East and almost as good.

Radio Stations:
WHRB. Harvard's excellent radio station.
WBCN. Somewhat slick alternative.
WMBR. A cutting-edge college station run by the Massachusetts Institute of Technology.
WFNX. Boston's commercial alternative station.

Record Stores:
In Your Ear. 1030 Commonwealth Avenue, Allston. 617-739-1236. A good alternative record shop, with a used section and a magazine and book section. They also have a Providence, Rhode Island, loca-tion.
Newbury Comics. 52 Everett St. 617-254-1666. A Boston-based chain of large, clean, well-stocked alternative record stores.

Local mags: *Boston Rock, Boston Phoenix.*

AUSTIN, TX
Clubs:
Liberty Lunch. 405 W. Second Street. 512-477-0461. The cool alter-native place to play in Austin. When Austin plays host to South By Southwest, an annual music industry convention, Liberty Lunch is the prime gig spot.
Steamboat. 403 E. 6th Street. 512-478-2912. Another venue which books alternative bands.

Radio Stations:
KTSB. Good college station, out of the University of Texas.
KNCC. A top-rate commercial alternative station.

Record Stores:
Waterloo: 600A N. Lamar Blvd. 512-474-2500. Highly recom-mended, excellent record store, with a good selection of vinyl and singles.

Local mags: *Austin Chronicle, Texas Monthly.*

SEATTLE

Clubs:

Backstage. 2208 Northwest Market Street. 206-789-1184. Small, cozy, and loud. A great place to see a band.

Radio Stations:

KCMU. An excellent, daring station out of the University of Washington.

KNND. A very good commercial alternative station.

Record Stores:

Fallout. 1506 E. Olive Way. 206-323-BOMB. Very cool record shop, which also features comics and skateboards.

Easy Street. 4559 California St. SW. 206-938-3279. Also recommended.

Cellophane Square. 1311 N.E. 42nd St. 206-634-2281. Another good alternative record store.

Local mags: *The Rocket, Seattle Weekly.*

NEW YORK

Clubs:

CBGB's. 315 Bowery. 212-982-4052. The gold standard of alternative clubs. Sure, it's grimy, but it's also where Television, the Ramones, and Blondie got their starts.

The Knitting Factory. 47 East Houston: 219-3006. Booking a diverse array of music, this is a good place to see a band.

Maxwell's. 1039 Washington St., Hoboken, N.J. 201-656-9632. It's out in Hoboken, New Jersey, but definitely worth the trip.

Radio Stations:

WDRE. A slick commercial alternative station which is a constant reminder of the lack of cutting-edge radio in New York.

WNYU. New York University's radio station, which is good, although it broadcasts for limited hours.

WFMU: Excellent, eclectic New Jersey station which comes into many New York households.

Record Stores:

Kim's Underground. 144 Bleecker St. 212-260-1010. A well-stocked, comprehensive selection of alternative records on major and independent labels as well as imports makes this the best alternative record shop in the city.

Rebel Rebel. 319 Bleecker St. 212-989-0770. This is a good place to find import albums and singles.

Pier Platters. 56 Newark Street, Hoboken. 201-795-4785. A surreal selection of alternative vinyl. This store is legendary, and lives up to the legend.

Local mags: *Village Voice, New York Press.*

PHILADELPHIA

Clubs:

J.C. Dobbs. 304 South Street. 215-925-4053. Too small for many of the cool bands which play here, along with Khyber Pass, which is nearby, this is one of the best places in town.

Trocadero. 1003 Arch Street. 215-592-0385. A big old theater where very successful alternative bands play.

Khyber Pass. 56 Second St. 215-440-9683. A tiny room to see alternative bands before they reach the masses-of-fans level.

Radio Stations:

WQHS. A good college station, based at the University of Pennsylvania.

WMMR. Philadelphia's commercial alternative station, owned by New York's WDRE.

WXPN. Good, varied alternative playlist.

Record Stores:

Record Cellar. 6032 Bustleton Ave. 215-624-1650. A well-stocked alternative record store.

3rd St. Rock and Jazz. 20 North Third Street. 215-627-3366. A good selection makes this one of the best shops in town.

Local mags: *City Paper.*

Clubs:
The Venue. 2A Clifton Rise, New Cross. 081-692-4077. Out of the way, but a comparatively large place to see alternative bands.
The Garage. 26/22 Highbury Corner. 071-607-1818. Another cool alternative space.
The Forum. 9-17 Highgate Road, Kentish Town. 071-284-2200. Formerly called the Town and Country, this venue is as comfortable as a club gets.

Radio Stations:
The essential alternative radio show in England is John Peel's, which is broadcast on weekend evenings on Radio One. Several other DJs have alternative taste, like Mark Goodier, but Peel is pretty much it.

Record Stores:
Rough Trade. 130 Talbot Road. 071-221-9717. This store stocks a wonderful selection of indie singles, albums, and t-shirts – and features a bulletin board where customers can post their handmade lists of current favorite releases. There is also a branch of Rough Trade in Covent Garden worth checking out.

Sister Ray. 94 Berwick Street. 071-287-8385. Another excellent store – and it's located right in the center of London.

Local mags: *NME* and *Melody Maker* (the weekly bibles of the alternative music scene), *Time Out, Q, Select.* All are available as imports in the United States.

LYRIC ACKNOWLEDGMENTS

Excerpts from the following songs are used by permission.

"How Soon Is Now?" by John Marr, Steven Morrissey. Copyright © 1984 Warner-Tamerlane Publishing Corp. All rights reserved.

"Half A Person" by Steven Morrissey, John Marr. Copyright © 1987 Warner-Tamerlane Publishing Corp. All rights reserved.

"Totally Wired" by The Fall. Copyright © 1980 Complete Music, Ltd. All rights reserved.

"C.R.E.E.P." by Brix Smith, Stephen Hanley, Paul Hanley, Craig Scanlon and Mark E. Smith. Copyright © 1984 by Minder Music. All rights reserved.

"New Face in Hell" by the Fall. Copyright © 1988 Minder Music. All rights reserved.

"Ladybird (Green Grass)" by the Fall. Copyright © 1993 Minder Music. All rights reserved.

"These Drinkers" by Kitchens of Distinction. Copyright © 1990 Tortoise Head Music/Main Lot Music. All rights reserved.

"Blue Pedal;" "On Tooting Broadway Station" by Kitchens of Distinction. Copyright © 1992 Tortoise Head Music/Main Lot Music. All rights reserved.

"The Sprawl" by Sonic Youth. Copyright © 1988 Savage Conquest Music. All rights reserved.

"JC;" "Swimsuit Issue;" "Drunken Butterfly" by Sonic Youth. Copyright © 1992 Sonik Tooth Music/Zomba Music Publishing. All rights reserved.

"Smells Like Teen Spirit;" "Come As You Are" lyrics by Kurt Cobain/music by Nirvana. Copyright © 1991 EMI Virgin Songs, Inc./The End of Music. All rights reserved.